Special Edition of

A Union Buster Confesses

An authorized reprint of select sections of
Confessions of a Union Buster

Martin Jay Levitt

**With comments from select
NJASAP members**

39PageGuidebooks
1866 Seclusion Dr
Port Orange Florida 32128

ISBN-10: 0991205677
ISBN-13: 978-0-9912056-7-7
Library of Congress PCN: 2014958592

Introduction

This book is specifically for the members of NJASAP*.

It is a Special Edition, edited from *A Union Buster Confesses*, the authorized reprint of the original book. *A Union Buster Confesses* is available in the full edition as both print and Kindle.

Why a Special Edition?

The original book is filled with personal circumstances of the author. Mr. Levitt's story is well worth the read from the full book. While excellent reading, the many details dilute the examples needed by this group.

This Special Edition for NJASAP members, however, is very highly refined to bring out as many examples as possible. Not the personal story of the original author, but the tricks, lies and deceit that are the common tools of union busters.

And these tactics are evident where we work. Today. The tactics are not new. But they may be new to you.

Perhaps you previously worked in an environment where management earned trust and confidence. Or maybe, like the military, no union was needed- although some militaries of the world do indeed have unions.

Sadly, our company appears willing to sacrifice safety, urges you make decisions that may put your license and future at risk, and has demonstrated little respect for the pilots, who are the face of the company, to those who pay the bills- the owners.

*The NJASAP Eboard cannot endorse the work of a member to avoid an accusation of conflict of interest.. Don't let that discourage or dissuade you from reading, learning, and applying the lessons.

This Special Edition is designed to open everyone's eyes.

To those who think they have seen it all, there is still new ground to cover.

To those who don't understand what is happening, here is the distilled version.

To those who believe there is nothing we can do, here are examples of people who rose up in the face of adversity.

No matter your reason for reading, each will grow.

Congratulations on taking a step toward the future.

How to read this book

What you are holding in your hand is intended to educate. There are three critical elements designed into this book to let everyone choose how they want to learn:

Element 1. The distilled chapters from "A Union Buster Confesses" that have significant points highlighted for emphasis and skimming.

Element 2. MembersSpeak® QR code links, those funny looking postage stamp sized ink blots. A scanning app from a smart device accesses comments from select NJASAP members who have taken the time to summarize the section.

Element 3. TheAuthorSpeaks® QR code links to actual video of the original author making points that the editors believe are most important to our struggle for a realistic contract.

There are also questions at the end of each section. These are to bring to mind examples in our everyday times on the road when some of the points of the chapter can be seen.

Disclaimer:

This book is assembled for educational purposes only.
The original author, his estate, any editors, contributors, interpreters, analysts, publishers, officers, employees, contractors, subcontractors and/or printers, named or unnamed- including anyone directly or tangentially associated with this project- assume no liability for any action by a reader based on him/her reading the contents of this publication whether in print or digital form. The original author, his estate, any editors, contributors, interpreters, analysts, publishers, officers, employees, contractors, subcontractors and/or printers will not accept liability for any injuries or damages to the reader that may result from the reader's acting upon or using the content contained in the publication.

No one associated with this work advocates violence, retribution, vengeance, retaliation, reprisal, payback, punishment or any type of illegal action by an individual or group.

Everyone associated with this work specifically advocates AGAINST any illegal work action.

The entire purpose of the book is to make the reader immune to the fear, uncertainty, doubt and intimidation discussed in the book.

By purchasing this work, you agree not to harass, offend, threaten, embarrass, distress or invade the privacy of any individual or entity.
You alone are responsible for your actions.

The editor asks…

How effective was Marty Levitt?

Can you trust he really knows the tricks and methods of a Union buster?

TheAuthorSpeaks®

Scan the code to listen or go to
http://bit.ly/1re5z8C

Scan this code with your smart device or type in the link to see the video. To see more of the author and hear his words, look for *"TheAuthorSpeaks®"* section in the center of the book. There are over 20 links like this, along with commonly asked questions that will give you the perspective you need to keep positive, unified, and motivated.

Prologue

Union busting is a field populated by bullies and built on deceit. A campaign against a union is an assault on individuals and a war on the truth. As such, it is a war without honor. The only way to bust a union is to lie, distort, manipulate, threaten, and always, always attack. The law does not hamper the process. Rather, it serves to suggest maneuvers and define strategies. Each "union prevention" campaign, as the wars are called, turns on a combined strategy of disinformation and personal assaults.

When a chief executive hires a labor relations consultant to battle a union, he gives the consultant run of the company and closes his eyes. The consultant, backed by attorneys, installs himself in the corporate offices and goes to work creating a climate of terror that inevitably is blamed on the union.

Some corporate executives I encountered liked to think of their anti-union consultants as generals. But really the consultants are terrorists. Like political terrorists, the consultants' attacks are in- tensely personal. Terrorists do not make factories and air strips their victims; they choose instead crippled old men and school- children. Likewise, as the consultants go about the business of destroying unions, they invade people's lives, demolish their friendships, crush their will, and shatter their families.

I entered the union -busting business in 1969 at age twenty-five. It wasn't an informed career choice, but a move motivated by ambition. I answered a blind ad in The Wall Street journal for a management consultant with knowledge of the National Labor Relations Act. I had never read a labor law, but I knew how to sell myself, so I sent off a resume to the post office box. At the time I answered the mystery ad, I had been running a successful executive recruitment firm for two years that did almost $100,000 in business annually, so I was pretty cocky. I had no biases for or against labor unions and no career goals save the desire to make money.

I was called to an interview with John Sheridan, a former union organizer from Chicago. His labor relations consulting firm, John Sheridan Associates, specialized in running campaigns to thwart union efforts to organize workers. I knew little about the work but was flattered to be considered for the job, so I put on my best show. Sheridan liked me from the start. My golden tongue won me a job with a starting billing rate of $250 a day.

Once I got a taste of the excitement, the power, the money, and the glamour in union busting, I was hooked. Right or wrong became irrelevant. It would be twenty years before I saw the field for what it is.

There are many forms of union busting. Some labor consultants, and attorneys take on unions that already represent a work force, squeezing negotiators at the bargaining table, forcing workers out on strike, harassing union officers. My career took another path. I refined the Sheridan specialty called "counter-organizing drives," battling non-union employees as they struggled to win union representation. The enemy was the collective spirit. I got hold of that spirit while it was still a seedling; I poisoned it, choked it, bludgeoned it if I had to, anything to be sure it would never blossom into a united work force, the dreaded foe of any corporate tyrant. For my campaigns I identified two key targets: the rank-and-file workers and their immediate supervisors. The supervisors served as my front line. I took them hostage on the first day and sent them to anti-union boot camp. I knew that people who didn't feel threatened wouldn't fight. So through hours of seminars, rallies, and one-on-one encounters, I taught the supervisors to despise and fear the union. I persuaded them that a union-organizing drive was a personal attack on them, a referendum on their leadership skills, and an attempt to humiliate them. I was friendly, even jovial at times, but always unforgiving as I compelled each supervisor to feel he was somehow to blame for the union push and consequently obliged to defeat it. Like any hostages, most supervisors could not resist for long. They soon came to see the fight through the eyes of their captor and went to work wringing union sympathies out of their workers.

Although I took on the supervisors face to face, my war on the union activists was covert.

To stop a union proponent- a "pusher," in the anti-union lexicon-the buster will go anywhere, not just to the lunch room, but into the bedroom if necessary .The buster not only is a terrorist; he is also a spy. My team and I routinely pried into workers' police records, personnel files, credit histories, medical records, and family lives in search of a weakness that we could use to discredit union activists.

Once in a while, a worker is impeccable. So some consultants resort to lies. To fell the sturdiest union supporters in the 1970s, I frequently launched rumors that the targeted worker was gay or was cheating on his wife. It was a very effective technique, particularly in blue-collar towns. If even the nasty stories failed to muzzle an effective union proponent, the busters might get the worker fired.

Such was the case of Jeannette Allen, an assembly-line worker at the Stant Company manufacturing plant outside Little Rock, Arkansas.

The Stant factory was torn by the conflict between a vigorous United Auto Workers organizing effort and a dogged counter-drive by corporate officers and their consultants. One night, as graveyard shift workers pressed and cut hot metal into the shape of radiator caps, the plant foreman's phone rang. The foreman answered and heard the voice of a black woman announce that there was a bomb in the factory. He then let the crew go on working for nearly an hour before evacuating the plant.

The police got a warning call from the same person that night. When they searched the factory they found nothing, but they had captured the caller's voice on tape. Two plant managers identified the caller as Allen. I believed it wasn't she. (When I heard the tape, I was sitting with Jeannette Allen herself. It did not sound like the same person.) A black woman whose intelligence and integrity had earned her the admiration and loyalty of her co-workers, Allen also happened to be an outspoken proponent of the UAW campaign. Company bosses, it seemed, considered her the driving force behind worker support for the union, particularly among blacks, who made up one third of the work force. They feared her. As soon as Allen was implicated in the bomb threat, she was fired. Meanwhile, her co-workers wondered what kind of union could corrupt such a stalwart character.

The UAW lost the election.

In 1975 I left the employ of consulting firms and set out on my own. Over the next eight years I ran a series of one-man union-busting enterprises I called by such disingenuous names as Employee Synthesis Program and

Human Resources Institute, and I struck it rich. But by 1983 I had become hopelessly alcoholic; the addiction had badly complicated my life, and solo work was taking its toll on me. I landed a counter-organizing job at an Ohio coal company five hundred workers strong, and I decided I needed backup. I called on some former colleagues from a Sheridan spin- off called Modern Management Methods and invited them to join me as I feasted off the carcass of the United Mine Workers. They did, gleefully, and my reaffiliation with MMM continued until the death of my shameful career.

Then the change started. Watching the crude and abusive behavior of my old associates during those years, I was forced to acknowledge the vile nature of my field. Slowly I began to realize that my more polished techniques were just a distilled version of the same villainy. Not only were working people crushed by the cruelty of the union busters, but the companies themselves were raped, as consultants and attorneys conspired to wring as much money as they could out of their clients. The executives paid whatever they were asked, the consultants having convinced them that a union-organizing effort amounted to the worst crisis of their business lives. In the end I understood that a union-busting campaign left a company financially devastated and hopelessly divided and almost invariably created an even more intolerable work environment than before, as managers systematically retaliated against union supporters for the high costs of the campaign. I felt repulsed by what I saw and sickened that I was, in fact, a prominent member of the club. I renounced the field.

My awakening came in late 1987. I was making $200,000 a year and living on a five-acre wooded estate in an exclusive community. I traveled, dined, and lodged in first class, drove only the finest luxury cars. By then I had directed more than two hundred anti-union campaigns- and lost only five- and had trained thousands of craven managers to go and do likewise at their own companies. I was at the top of my field, one of the best and one of the richest. No, I was not driven from the field by need. I was driven by horror and remorse.

As labor laws have proliferated, the arena of employee relations and contract negotiations has become infinitely more complicated; more and more professionals have built their careers on advising employers how to manage their work force and cope with the maze of federal and state worker laws. Some such professionals clearly are needed, and a few even do an honest job. But within the field of labor relations the big money is in union busting. When I entered the field, only a handful of law firms and consulting companies specialized in combating worker organizations. Today there are more than seven thousand attorneys and consultants across the nation who make their living busting unions, and they work almost every day. At a billing rate of $1,000 to $1,500 a day per consultant and $300 to $700 an hour for attorneys, the war on organized labor is a $1 billion-plus industry.

(Editor's note: In 2014 dollars, approximately $1600-$2500 per DAY and $500-$1100 per HOUR for attorneys)

Many consultants have given up union busting and quietly gone about building more honorable careers for themselves, sort of like former Nazis moving to America and setting up flower shops. Not I. At the time I made my conversion, I was struggling to overcome alcoholism. In my pursuit of recovery I also sought redemption, so I came to believe it was my moral duty to confront what I had done and somehow to make amends to my tens of thousands of victims. At that moment I vowed I would do whatever I could to stop the others in my trade from carrying out their hateful mission. I would not run and hide.

I placed a call to the AFL-CIO office in Washington, D.C., and spoke to Virginia Diamond, then a labor federation attorney who tracked the activities of more than five hundred union-busting firms across the nation in a publication called the *RUB Sheet* (for "report on union busters"). I told Diamond that she had one less union buster to worry about. That conversation led indirectly to my new vocation, as a consultant to unions on how to bust the busters.

Not long after my change of heart became the talk of labor circles, the United Auto Workers called me to testify as an expert witness in Jeannette Allen's wrongful termination suit against Stant Company. I immediately recognized the bomb threat ploy as a typical union buster's dirty trick, and I said so in court. I believed the voice on the police tape was not Allen's; after all, the company never prosecuted her, they just got her out of the way. I was convinced some of Stant's consultants had hatched the bomb scare scheme when their anti-union campaign was on the verge of collapse.

It was a contemptible plan. But it was a perfect one by the only measure that matters in the war on labor: it worked.

A page from the Editor:

Want a short background on Union Busting?

This summary, from Marty Levitt, is from the original text for those who want to understand that union busting has a deep history.

The tactics, tricks, fear, uncertainty and doubt are all orchestrated based on years of refining.

Although history, this section is highly recommended reading to understand that some of the tricks, such as the use of language to hide the methods, can be traced to the 1930s.

And this summary ends in 1969- almost 45 years ago. But the tricks are as current today as ever.

Link to the QR below to get applications to our current situation.

The Editor

MembersSpeak®

Scan the code to listen or go to
http://bit.ly/1nIYaOcAv

Genesis

The field called preventive labor relations got its start the moment labor organizations gained legal sanction, with the passage of the National Labor Relations Act in 1935. The law, popularly known as the Wagner Act, established the right of employees to organize in order to negotiate collectively with their employer over wages, hours, benefits, and working conditions and to otherwise fight for their combined interests. The primary labor component of Franklin D. Roosevelt's New Deal, the Wagner Act also outlawed many employer tactics then commonly used to break unions-most notoriously, spying on and intimidating union activists, provoking violence, and enticing workers into management-controlled "company unions" in order to stifle their call for independent labor organizations. The new law defined such activities, and many others, as unfair labor practices and created the National Labor Relations Board to oversee and enforce its provisions. Passage of the Wagner Act clearly was a victory for workers, but they hardly had time for celebration, for the law itself set off a vigorous countermovement among employers and their attorneys. With federal law recognizing workers' rights to self-organization and collective bargaining, many of the old union -busting tactics would have to be traded in for more subtle techniques. Among employers there grew a great demand for expertise in the tricks of what was called "union avoidance." All that was needed were a few good capitalists ready to tap that burgeoning market, and a whole new industry was born.

The first nationally known management consulting firm that specialized in helping companies evade unions was Labor Relations Associates of Chicago, Inc. Labor Relations Associates was formed in 1939, just two years after the U.S. Supreme Court upheld the Wagner Act and ordered its full implementation. The firm was founded by a veteran personnel man named Nathan Shefferman, a member of the original National Labor Relations Board in 1934, who a year later became director of employee relations at Sears, Roebuck & Co. Today perhaps few people recognize the name Shefferman. But when Shefferman's company folded in 1959 after twenty years in business, his name and that of his firm had become forever linked with the more shameful elements of organized labor. That year,

Shefferman was charged with conspiring to help Teamsters president Dave Beck avoid paying income taxes.

Although the charge against Shefferman was dropped, Beck was prosecuted and convicted; Shefferman's longtime association with Beck, and thus with the dark side of organized labor, would not be forgotten. Beck was convicted of three union-related financial crimes: income tax evasion, grand larceny, and filing false union income tax return s. The only conviction to stick, however, was for filing tax returns; the other two were dropped and pardoned, respectively. Beck served thirty months of a five-year sentence.

Throughout the 1930s Sears was engaged in continuous battle to block unions from the retail industry. The Chicago-based chain carried out a particularly vicious, ongoing war with the Teamsters union, which was attempting to organize drivers and other workers at several companies that supplied merchandise and distribution services to Sears. Sears's executives were uncompromising; with the help of Shefferman they had managed successfully to ward off the unions on both fronts in the pre-Wagner Act years. But union organizing, active throughout the 1930s, turned relentless after passage of the Wagner Act, and the countermeasures needed to defeat the unions became infinitely more complex. For those reasons, by 1939 Shefferman's anti-union duties so dominated his work at Sears that he set up a separate company to handle the union-evasion business. With seed money from Sears in the form of a $10,000 retainer, Labor Relations Associates was born.

Enter a family named Lederer. Handling the legal logistics of forming Labor Relations Associates was a Chicago law firm called Lederer, Livingston, Kahn & Adsit, primary counsel to Sears. The Lederer on the masthead, Charles Lederer, had served as one of Sears's lead attorneys almost since the formation of the company in 1906. When his son, Philip, got his law degree, the father brought the younger man aboard. For nineteen years Phil Lederer practiced law with his father. He started out helping Dad with his duties as Sears general counsel, but later on the younger Lederer got himself some training in labor relations and won an appointment as chief labor attorney for the Sears Corporation. And where did Philip train? At the offices of Nathan Shefferman and Labor Relations Associates, of course. As Phil explains it, he dropped out of the law for a bit during World War II to bone up on employee relations and thus possibly win a commission to the navy as a personnel expert. The commission never came through; instead Phil spent the war years working as a consultant for Labor Relations Associates -taking the place of other consultants who were called to military service-and learning the back-room tricks of the burgeoning preventive labor relations trade. Although he was functioning as an on-site consultant at the time, not an attorney, Phil was called upon by several management attorneys to argue cases on their behalf before the National War Labor Board, created by Franklin Roosevelt to arbitrate labor disputes during the war in return for a no-strike pledge from labor. By VE Day Phil Lederer had developed a solid grasp of both labor law and anti-union personnel theory.

After the Second World War, Phil Lederer went back to a busy law practice. Throughout the next decade and a half he worked in close harmony with Labor Relations Associates, where business was flourishing in a climate of renewed anti-unionism. The war ended, corporate America had unleashed an angry anti-labor propaganda drive. At the time, Shefferman was building a daunting business on a foundation of false premises; the same silent assertions that continue to serve as the dogma of anti-union consultants, lawyers, and business managers. Perhaps the most incredible-and most widely believed- is the myth that companies are at a disadvantage to unions organizationally, legally, and financially during a union organizing drive. In the postwar furor, business leaders characterized unions as fat, greedy, corrupt, and decidedly un-American. They demanded that Congress amend the Wagner Act, complaining that the law gave unions an insurmountable advantage over management. Executives charged that by protecting unions, but not management, from improper practices during organizing drives and elections, the Wagner Act allowed unions to be coercive, to threaten, and to intimidate workers at will. They just wanted to level the playing field. In 1947 Congress bowed to management's wishes. After a prolonged and stormy debate, conservative Congressmen won passage of a sweeping labor reform law, overriding the veto by President Harry S Truman, who condemned the law as designed primarily to weaken unions. Commonly referred to as the Taft-Hartley Act, the 1947 law attacks unions on almost every front. To this day union leaders consider the Taft-Hartley Act a primary cause of labor's failure to organize the majority of American workers. Among the law's most significant provisions are the establishment of unfair labor practices that can be charged against unions; a listing of specific "employer rights" available to management during union-organizing efforts, including a broad freedom of expression; an outright ban on the closed shop, in which union membership is a precondition of employment; and an open invitation to states to pass even more restrictive legislation. One provision, since removed from the law, required union officers to file affidavits proclaiming that they had no affiliation to the Communist party. Taft-Hartley was devastating to labor. It led to a proliferation of state legislation disingenuously called "right to work" laws, which prohibit mandatory union dues; perpetuated the red baiting that already haunted the labor movement; and loaded management's union-busting arsenal with complicated restrictions on fundamental union activities. Executives and their consultants knew that with the Taft-Hartley amendments in place, employers would enjoy freedom in combating worker organizations. Management always had the upper hand, of course; they had never lost it. But thanks to Taft-Hartley, the bosses could once again wage their war with near impunity.

Labor law grew more complex almost by the day in the 1940s and 1950s, and good attorneys were at a premium. Phil Lederer, it would seem, was in the right place at just the right time. During the postwar years, Lederer worked as Sears chief labor counsel, not only taking charge of all labor matters at the mother company, but handling as well the labor relations and civil rights cases for Allstate Insurance Co., a Sears subsidiary. A little more than a decade later, Lederer's insurance connection would provide the spark that ignited a firm named John Sheridan Associates, my first union-busting employer. But before that, labor was to suffer yet another legislative catastrophe.

Almost from its inception American organized labor has had to combat a grave public image problem. Violence against employers and union members alike, reports of Communist infiltration into the labor movement, and evidence of union ties to organized crime plagued labor leaders and provided their enemies with strategic weapons for destroying their cause. The Wagner Act had helped tame the violence by the late 1930s, and labor leaders worked feverishly during the 1940s to purge their ranks of avowed Communists. But within some of the nation's largest and most powerful unions, racketeering persisted, and labor's mob connection grew more entrenched. By 1957 organized labor seemed so rife with corruption that the Senate appointed a special subcommittee to investigate allegations of criminal activities. The committee, headed by Senator John McClellan of Arkansas, boasted such lofty membership as John F. Kennedy, then a young senator from Massachusetts, and had as its chief counsel a youthful Robert F. Kennedy. The televised hearings stunned Americans with its revelations of rigged union elections, collusion of union leaders and employers, embezzlement, and theft. One of the chief targets of the Senate investigations was the Teamsters union, and the committee found evidence of corruption at nearly every level, up to the international president, Dave Beck. Beck had been elected president of the Teamsters in 1952 on a promise to clean up the union. But five years later witnesses testified before the McClellan Anti-Racketeering Committee that Beck was diverting large amounts of union funds for his own purposes, misappropriations that included payments to Labor Relations Associates. Largely as a result of the hearings, Beck was convicted of tax evasion and grand larceny; his successor, the notorious Jimmy Hoffa, was convicted and jailed for jury tampering and mail fraud; and the Teamsters union was expelled from the AFL-CIO.

Although the McClellan Committee concentrated on the misdeeds of organized labor, the senators also took a peek behind management's doors. What they found was no less disturbing. For two and a half weeks the committee heard testimony about improper management practices; for several days they focused on the dealings of one man, Nathan Shefferman. By the mid-1950s Shefferman's firm, Labor Relations Associates, boasted three hundred clients from coast to coast and was probably the largest employee relations consulting business in the nation. Witness testimony, combined with information gathered during an investigation led by congressional aide Pierre Salinger, showed Labor Relations Associates to be a very lucrative and clearly unethical enterprise: Shefferman's battalion of consultants traveled the country, using whatever tactics they could get away with to keep employees of client companies from joining unions. According to hearings transcripts, those means included conniving with local labor officials; manipulating union elections through bribery and coercion; threatening to revoke workers' benefits should they organize; installing union officers sympathetic to management; offering to reward employees who worked against the union; and spying on and harassing workers- all clearly illegal under federal labor law. Named in the testimony as one of Shefferman's consultants was one Herbert Melnick.

When the McClellan Committee hearings ended in 1959, the American public was left with a dreary portrait of U.S. business and labor. As McClellan himself said at the close of the testimony concerning Shefferman: "The activities disclosed before this committee reflect a great discredit on some business firms in this country." The committee vigorously condemned the shenanigans of many labor unions, but they took U.S. management to task as well. Said McClellan, "[I]t was the services which management desired which created the need for Nathan Shefferman. It was management who paid the bills for the activities of Nathan Shefferman, and it was management that knowingly utilized the services of Nathan Shefferman with no compunctions or regrets until the revelations in recent months. They were aware of what they were doing and how their money was being utilized."

Following the hearings, Beck was sent to prison; meanwhile Congress went to work on a law to regulate the internal practices of unions and thus stem the tide of corruption.

In 1961, two years after Labor Relations Associates dissolved in shame, Shefferman published a book entitled *The Man in the Middle*, a 292-page justification of his four decades in anti-union employee relations work. In the book Shefferman whines a great deal about his treatment before the McClellan Committee and defends his work ad nauseam. His key defense lay in his claim that union avoidance constituted "a tiny percentage" of his labor relations work. By way of illustration, he cites a laundry list of other personnel services he provided, as reported by one client to the McClellan Committee. The list included the administration of opinion surveys, supervisor training, incentive pay procedures, wage surveys, employee complaints, personnel records, application procedures, job evaluations, and legal services. The other services were rendered, to be sure. But the truth is, if union busting was part of the work, then the entire package was tainted. Everything else had to be performed in concert with the overall goal of keeping top management in complete control. Every other piece of a company's employee relations work had a part in that drama. To borrow a line from Shefferman's own book: "So we find that even the hidden thread is basic to the fabric of labor-management relations."

In Shefferman's labor relations' work can be found the seeds of all subsequent union-busting techniques, as well as the language employed to shroud the deeds. He is the true godfather of modern union busting. Shefferman laid the bedrock of the industry. He designed scores of strategies for countering unions, techniques that formed the core of his work-and later mine -and that continue to dominate labor relations. But Shefferman's contribution was much greater than his repertoire of tactics. We have Shefferman to thank, perhaps more than anyone else, for the development of a magnificently insidious doublespeak that persists in labor- management theory to this day. The language of employee relations as articulated by Shefferman and the thousands he influenced masks a fundamental distrust of workers and a view of management as defenders of the crown, with words and schemes that seem to promote the opposite . It is easy to fall for the words; the ideas are beautiful. In his 1961 book Shefferman wags a finger at paternalistic bosses; calls for managers to recognize workers' individuality; promotes continual two-way communication between management and workers; and challenges bosses to respect their employees' dignity.

So what's the problem? The problem is unions. Mix the fear of unions into management's employee relations potion and the result is poison –a poison so potent that it contaminates even the most seemingly altruistic plan. Every program, every new workplace strategy, is twisted, inverted, perverted into a tactic for undermining the collective spirit of workers.

Here is an example from the Shefferman school of subterfuge: Under the real or even theoretical threat of a union, Shefferman advised management to institute a device called an employee roundtable. Purportedly designed to give workers a way to air their grievances and influence company policy, in reality the roundtable becomes management's tap into the worker grapevine and its repressive thumb on the informal worker power structure. The regular group meetings provided management with a system for planting information, as well as for identifying and controlling the leaders among employees. Shefferman lays out the blueprint for such roundtables in his book. Calling them "rotating employee committees," he presents the sessions as open forums, absent any supervisors, opportunities for workers to gripe without fear of reprisal. But the fact is, such committees serve management's interests more directly than the needs of the workers. The operative word here is "rotating." Shefferman, no fool, advised management to steer clear of programs that could foster in workers a group identity. He boasts in his book, for example, that he took the contrary view in admonishing Sears executives against the formation of a company union during the 1920s, when many firms were using employee associations as a shield against true labor organizations. Shefferman says he argued that the company-union strategy could backfire by teaching employees how to work in concert and thus ma king them more susceptible to an independent union.

In his book Shefferman doesn't spell out the reason for the rotating participation in the employee committees. Bur his students—who later became my teachers—learned it well and passed it along: by continually changing the makeup of the employee committee, management could keep abreast of complaints and rumors circulating in the various departments without creating a bond among the participants or inadvertently developing leaders. The goal was to foster cooperation between employees and management, not among the employees themselves. In tandem with the gripe sessions, Shefferman prescribed a very intricate supervisor training course. Each front-line supervisor, whom he refers to as the sub management, would be taught to identify and analyze the power relationships among his subordinates, in order to focus his coercive energy on the workers with the greatest influence and thus more efficiently control the attitudes and behavior of the whole group.

Although I scarcely recognized the name Shefferman when I entered the union-busting business, ten, twenty, even thirty years later I was promoting a very similar system to my clients as a long-term union-repellent strategy.

While Dave Beck was preparing to go to prison, President Dwight Eisenhower signed into law the Landrum-Griffin Act. The nation's little cadre of labor consultants cheered. Landrum-Griffin, officially the Labor-Management Reporting and Disclosure Act of 1959, contains five major sections, including a Bill of Rights for union members designed to make unions more democratic and open, particularly with regard to union funds. What gave labor consultants glee were the financial provisions, which required unions to file a copy of their constitution and rules with the secretary of labor and to file yearly financial reports, and compelled union officers and employees to report any financial transactions involving themselves or their family members that might constitute a conflict of interest. Wow. Union busters couldn't have asked for a bigger break. For the first time, detailed, timely information on the inner workings and finances of unions and labor leaders would be available to consultants and attorneys for the price of a photocopy. Thank you, Congress.

The Landrum-Griffin regulations were not aimed solely at unions, however. The McClellan Committee was clearly disturbed by the tactics used by employers and their consultants in their fight against unions, and Congress addressed the scandal in Landrum-Griffin. In order to place companies' anti-union efforts under public scrutiny, the law requires companies to report to the secretary of labor certain expenditures related to their anti-union activities, including the hiring of labor relations consultants. And the consultants must report the terms and conditions of their contract with the company and reveal the amount of money received. Had it not been for a couple of well-placed loopholes, those disclosure provisions could have snuffed out the anti-union consulting industry in its infancy. A master of illusion, the union buster pulls off his tricks amid the confusion of smoke and mirrors; his magic disappears under the blazing lights of center stage.

But the loopholes in Landrum-Griffin are shameful-enormous, gaping errors in the law that have left room for a sleazy billion-dollar industry to plod through without even sucking in its bloated middle. The law states that management consultants only have to file financial disclosures if they engage in certain kinds of activities, essentially attempting to persuade employees not to join a union or supplying the employer with information regarding the activities of employees or a union in connection with a labor relations matter. Of course, that is precisely what anti-union consultants do, have always done. Yet I never filed with Landrum-Griffin in my life, and few union busters do. Here's why not: According to the law, in order to be considered engaging in "persuader" activities, the consultant must speak directly to the employees in the voting unit. As long as he deals directly only with supervisors and management, he can easily slide out from under the scrutiny of the Department of Labor, which collects the Landrum-Griffin reports.

A handful of labor consultants do file; since they do not mask their efforts to convince workers to vote against the union and therefore are legally classified as "persuaders," not to file would set off an alarm over at the IRS. But they know well that the Labor Department has no reliable method for checking the accuracy of the reports. The consultants' role as spy is similarly protected by Landrum-Griffin loopholes. All kinds of information gathering is allowed to go on with no disclosure consequences if the information is to be used solely for a specific legal proceeding. Of course, we consultants wouldn't limit the fruits of our espionage to use in a single court case, but it is easy enough to make it appear that way. With the help of our trusted attorneys, our anti-union activities were carried out in backstage secrecy; meanwhile we gleefully showcased every detail of union finances that could be twisted into implications of impropriety or incompetence. Helping all this along is Landrum-Griffin's ambiguous treatment of attorneys. It is not clear under the law whether labor lawyers should be bound by the same reporting requirements as anti-union consultants, even when they perform similar duties, as they often do. Attorneys therefore can get away with direct interference in the union-organizing process without being forced to disclose their deeds or the corresponding fees. It is common in large labor law firms today to send out the junior associates to do the kind of work I once did for companies. Sheltered by the broad umbrella of attorney-client privilege, the young lawyers run bold anti-union wars and dance all over Landrum-Griffin.

Two former consultants from Labor Relations Associates, John Sheridan and Herbert Melnick, were shrewd enough to know that the best defense against Landrum-Griffin was to be found within the law itself. Using the language of the law as a blueprint, the two designed a daring new approach to union busting and recast the entire industry. The seed for the plan had been planted by Shefferman himself: during four decades of personnel work, Shefferman had pegged front-line supervisors as the most effective lobbyists for management, and he had teamed up with labor attorneys to fight unions. It was just one small step from there to a system of anti-union campaigning built on the legal specialness of those two groups.

While the labor world was still reeling from Landrum-Griffin, Sheridan and Melnick swam ashore from the sinking Labor Relations Associates ship and teamed up to start a consulting business of their own. They rented an office in downtown Chicago and went to work trying to sell their new concept. Rather than peddle their services directly to companies, Sheridan and Melnick called on attorneys and pitched their work as a complement to the duties of labor lawyers. The duo argued that together, attorneys and consultants could orchestrate a double-barreled attack on union drives and thus outmuscle and outwit the unions while staying out of reach of Landrum-Griffin. The arrangement also would provide a constant source of work for both the attorneys and the consultants, with each side continually referring work to the other. It was a brilliant plan. Few law firms appreciated the opportunity at first, but Sheridan landed the one that counted-Lederer, Fox & Grove, Phil Lederer's firm.

It so happened there was a great deal of organizing activity in the insurance industry at the time, and Phil Lederer had plenty of insurance clients who wanted help battling the unions. Lederer knew Melnick from his days with Labor Relations Associates, had brought him in on an anti-union job at Allstate, and he liked the spunk and style of Jack Sheridan. The tripartite combination was a winner. Lederer describes the alliance succinctly: "I would bring two of them in to do the consulting work, while I did the legal work. I did not try to run the campaigns against the unions .I pretty much stuck to the law."

Thanks to Lederer's experience, not to mention his rich and loyal client base, Sheridan's business prospered. It wasn't long before there was more work than the two could handle. And so the Sheridan expansion began. In 1969 John Sheridan Associates took on a rookie union buster named Marty Levitt.

Have you participated in an 'employee roundtables' here?

Have you seen any of the generic methods Levitt talks about here during your tours?

Do you believe that management is really listening during recurrent classes?

A page from the Editor:

What does a coal mine have in common pilots and aviation?

Surprisingly, a lot.

In this section, summarized by a NJASAP member via the QR code below, the many methods used at this coal mine years ago are mirrored in our struggle. Although this is an organizing effort, the parallels are obvious.

Use of supervisors to sway and intimidate, destruction of families, and paying large sums to union busters solely for the ego of management are seen here.

Each QR code connects to either video or audio of the actual author, Martin Jay Levitt.

The highlighted sections each cover a specific type or method.

Can you identify how these methods are used against us today?

The Editor

MembersSpeak®

Scan the code to listen or go to
http://bit.ly/1rB1UBL

Cravat Coal

The sticky Ohio summer heat had given way to autumn's chill. A miner I'll call Ha l Lockett fixed his hunting rifle in its rack on the back of his dust-covered Dodge pickup, gave the bald rear tires a kick, and climbed into the cab. His eyes were as cold as the coal he had been digging since dawn every morning practically since he was a baby-cold as the coal Lockett's daddy mined and his grand- daddy before him. But Lockett's heart was burning. Two months had gone by since a handful of well-dressed strangers had walked into the converted roadside motel that housed the offices of Cravat Coal Company, bearing poison and promises. In those two months Lockett had stopped believing. Men who had worked together like brothers for years-some were brothers, for chrissakes-had started taking blows at each other's heads and saying nasty things about each other's wives. Some had stopped talking altogether. Lockett still wasn't sure who those strangers were. He knew they'd showed up just a few weeks after the guy from United Mine Workers had come around asking people to sign little yellow cards and saying the union would help the miners keep their jobs and make sure they could afford to see a doctor. Sure, Lockett knew all about chat. That's what his daddy had told him, too. But somehow the whole thing had just gotten crazy. His foreman, usually a nice guy, had taken to badgering the men, threatening them, questioning them, and telling them didn't they know they'd lose everything if they let that goddamned union in. The workers were so divided, some couldn't stand next to each other in the pit without starting a fight.

Lockett kept his eyes straight ahead as he drove the winding road from the mine to a converted farmhouse at the edge of the gritty town of Cadiz, whose sole and incongruous fame rested in having been the birthplace of Clark Gable. Lockett drove the pickup practically into the side of the ramshackle building, one of the six Cravat field offices, slammed on the brakes, and shut off the motor. Inside, half a dozen secretaries tapped away at their mundane tasks. Lockett walked slowly to the back of the truck, lifted his rifle from its rack, and released the safety. He pushed open the door of the farmhouse and stomped inside. Then a one-man war broke out. Unintelligible curses streamed from Lockett's mouth as his free hand grabbed paperweights, staplers, and file folders from nearby desks and hurled them across the room. He gave his weapon a quick cock and squeezed the trigger. One shot rang out. Then another. Then another. Lockett tore through the building, pumping bullets out the windows and into the ceiling. A secretary screamed and dove under her desk. Then a man's voice was heard: "What the hell? Stop him!" Lockett blasted away, sobbing and raging all the time.

By the time the Cadiz police arrived, Lockett's face was stained with tears and mud. His eyes had lost their focus. No one was hurt, but a handful of townspeople and Cravat office workers had gathered for the spectacle. They knew the rifleman as a veteran miner out at one of Cravat's most remote pits. Everyone knew the union business had been getting to him, poor guy. He had enough trouble, with his marriage on the rocks and all. People had been talking about it for weeks. The police loaded a subdued Lockett into the car and drove off to the station. This was no good.

I first met Cravat Coal on paper. One hot August day in 1983, I sent the paralegal student who worked as my assistant to the National Labor Relations Board office in downtown Cleveland to poke through the filings. That was the method I had developed to generate work during slow times. It turned out to be a brilliant tactic, for of ten I discovered a union-organizing drive before company executives had any suspicions. The timeliness of my call made it impossible to ignore, and the chief executives' panic allowed me to suggest that, having caught the trouble early, we could launch our offensive while the union was still struggling to develop a strategy. That, in fact, was the case with Cravat. My student-assistant had discovered a union representation petition that had been filed just a day before by the United Mine Workers District 6, based in Wheeling, in neighboring West Virginia. The UMWA aimed to organize the 485 miners at what was then the nation's largest independent coal-mining company.

I gave Cravat a call. The call reached Mike Puskarich, the eldest of the four Yugoslavian-American brothers who, with their sons, ran Cravat Coal and a handful of related businesses.

"Mr. Puskarich, I'm Marty Levitt, president of Human Resources Institute of Cleveland. I thought you should know that your company has become the victim of a union-organizing campaign by United Mine Workers. Were you aware of that?"

He wasn't. But it didn't take Puskarich long to let me know where he stood: He wasn't going to have any fuckin' union, that was for goddamned sure. They had tried this shit before, he told me. Well, they were not going to get away with it.

That, of course, was the entree I needed. I kept my language polished but my message rough as I pressed Puskarich. "If you're intent on beating the union, we should get together as soon as possible," I told him.

Puskarich wasn't sure. He didn't go in for outside consultants, liked to handle problems himself. He had an in-house attorney who could stifle any union shenanigans. I told Puskarich he might not be aware of how deadly a United Mine Workers organizing drive could be. If he lost the union election, there'd be no turning back, no recovering the days when he was boss of his own company. I recommended he talk to a labor lawyer I had worked with for several years, a brilliant attorney by the name of Earl Leiken. Puskarich said he'd meet with me the next day.

The drive down to Cadiz was a trip into another decade. The town of four thousand souls stood nestled in the scarred hills of the flattened Appalachians in eastern Ohio. There was only one highway through Cadiz, and the peculiar Cravat Coal building stood off that road like a camp symbol that the town was somehow lost in space and time. The long, two-story brick structure retained the sterile and prim look it must have had as a motel. The conversion to corporate offices seemed halfhearted, for secretaries and clerks could be seen roaming the outdoor hallways carrying papers and coffee from one executive to another, like motel maids.

When I found myself before General Manager Mike Puskarich, I understood that this anti-union campaign would be like no other. Puskarich was a hulk of a man, a 250-pound beast with bushy eyebrows, massive forearms, and huge, rough hands. I likened him in my mind to the late hard-line Soviet Leonid Brezhnev, then at the helm of the Communist party. Puskarich's long-sleeved starched white shirt and gilded cuff links looked out of place; his thick fingers were adorned with gold-and-diamond rings. Puskarich's language was crude, his temper explosive; as I sat across from him and explained my strategy, I could see that he was not a man of subtleties. Instinctively I knew the Puskariches would be a liability in an anti-union fight built on subtle distortions and manipulations. I knew I would have to rein in the Yugoslavians' tempers lest they give the union promoters more fuel for the organizing campaign.

As I explained my strategy, I watched Puskarich fidget. He was not used to this kind of talk. "The entire campaign," I told him, "will be run through your foremen. I'll be their mentor, their coach. I'll teach them what to say and make sure they say it. But I'll stay in the background. This will be a case of over-communication. I will make the foremen feel they have post doctorate degrees in labor relations before this is through. They'll fill their employees with so many nasty little facts about unions, they'll all wish they'd never let this get started."

Puskarich wasn't sure. He had never thought of foremen as management. The only management was the Puskarich clan. The foremen were just a bunch of stupid miners, grunts like all the rest and not to be trusted. How could he count on them to take on the union for him? Hell, they'd probably called the union themselves. "You'll have to do it," he commanded.

I objected. Think about it, I said. How could I come in, an outsider, and convince the workers not to trust another outsider? My anti-union message would turn on portraying the union as a power-hungry interloper, and nobody was going to buy it coming from the company's hired gun. No, the words and the warnings would have to come from people they worked with every day down in the pits, from the people they counted on for that good review and that weekly paycheck.

"Here's how it is," I told Puskarich, fixing a steady gaze on his angry eyes. "You'll come to see this union drive as a blessing in disguise. Once our campaign gets rolling, supervisors will learn to be the leaders they should have been all along. They'll learn to make their people happy and to love what they do. The men won't just be working for a paycheck anymore, and you'll never face another union problem again."

Puskarich couldn't be persuaded by such a high-road argument, I knew, but I decided to throw it in to make the Cravat attorney happy. I wanted him on my side. I warned Puskarich that I would do some unusual things throughout the campaign; some activities he might find offensive, others corny. He brushed aside the warning. His only doubt had to do with embracing his foremen as allies. "We'll convince the foremen that when the National Labor Relations Board holds the representation election, the workers will not be voting for or against the union, but for or against the management, including all of them," I told the Yugoslav. "To lose the election would be a humiliation, an indictment of their management abilities. Once they see it my way, the foremen will gladly join the war on the UMWA.

Puskarich started to growl, but his attorney silenced him: "Listen to the man. We need him."

The boss lifted a diamond-studded hand to his fleshy face, twisted his mouth, and asked my fee. It was $1,000 a day per consultant-I planned to use several-plus a $10,000 retainer. Puskarich complained, "I've never known anybody worth a thousand a day." Then he barked at his secretary, Dottie, to make me out a check for $10,000. He offered his hand and commanded, "You're in charge."

During that first meeting, there were lots of logistics to map out. I insisted on holding the kick-off meeting in just two days; I didn't want the union to gain momentum while we chewed on our pencils. Cadiz was an uncomfortable four-and-a-half -hour drive from Cleveland, so naturally I was to stay in town during the week. Puskarich put me up in the best there was, ·a Sheraton hotel in a neighboring town. But even better was his weekend shuttle service. Every Friday evening throughout the seventeen-week campaign, he had the company plane fly me to the Cuyahoga County airport near my home in Gates Mills in suburban Cleveland, just a half hour away by air. Every Monday morning the plane picked me up and delivered me to Cadiz, where a company car awaited my arrival.

From the moment I read the UMWA petition for Cravat, I knew we faced a bitter fight. The key to my so-called union- prevention campaigns had always been to paint the labor organization as a greedy outsider and to convince supervisors and foremen that their jobs depended on its destruction. Meanwhile I worked to recast upper management with a human face-now silly, now generous, but always very human-so workers would come to believe there was no need for a union. In the UMWA I had a particularly formidable foe; not that the miner's union was more honorable or more sophisticated or even more aggressive than any other. But to miners, the UMWA was more than a union. It was family. Some of the workers at Cravat were the first in three generations not to belong to the UMWA, and they were not happy about it. The only other major mining concern in Cadiz was R&F Coal Company down the road from the Cravat headquarters, another non-union outfit owned by the mammoth Shell Oil Company. In effect, the union had been locked out of the town. Yet among miners, to speak against the union was a sacrilege. Federal law blesses a union-organizing drive if 30 percent of the workers sign authorization cards inviting the union in. At Cravat, 80 percent of the miners had signed. How was I going to get people to fight a union they had been brought up to think of as the Mother Church?

I was convinced I shouldn't tackle Cravat on my own, so I called for help from four former colleagues at a Chicago-based labor-consulting firm called Modern Management Methods, or Three M. By 1983 the union-busting field was bursting, and it was easy to find eager ass kickers in need of work. Joining me at the Cravat bloodletting were Tom Crosbie, an executive vice-president at Three M and my onetime mentor; Ed Juodenas, a large, imposing figure and a fifteen-year veteran of the ignoble trade; Dennis Fisher, a meticulous, soft-spoken methods man; and Kevin Smyth, an intense, portly man with a look of malevolence in his eyes. The firepower added by those union-buster heavyweights was phenomenal. Yet the aggressiveness of Cravat's union activists turned the Cravat war into one of the bloodiest of my career. By the time the defeat of the union was history, six Cravat foremen had been fired; one rank-and-file miner had gone crazy; at least one miner's marriage was in trouble because of unsavory rumors floated by the buster forces; and countless Cravat families and friendships were shattered as the entire population of southeastern Ohio chose sides. The intensity of loyalty to the UMWA dictated that we use every tool available to divide the miners. One-on-one interviews with foremen would be the heart of the counter union drive, as usual, but attorney Leiken, my fellow experts, and I knew we could begin our sabotage even before the first meeting. We needed just one tool, the National Labor Relations Act of 1935.

It so happens that the NLR Act, the bible of collective bargaining, can be a union buster's best friend. In its complexity the nation's fundamental labor law presents endless possibilities for delays, roadblocks, and maneuvers that can undermine a union's efforts and frustrate would-be members. In a bit of classic union- buster irony, we divided the Cravat workers by forcing them together. Cravat ran a handful of businesses in addition to its twenty-five Ohio mines: three trucking firms, a fuels company, a couple of quarries, a farm, and a Kentucky coal-mining concern called Blue Grass Mining. Only the Ohio miners had been approached by the UMWA, and we were betting that workers in other divisions could be turned against the union, particularly if we got to them first.

Our first legal move, then, was to petition the National Labor Relations Board in Cleveland to expand the UMWA voting unit to include all Cravat workers. Leiken was an opaque, colorless personality, but when it came to forming legal arguments, he was a genius. The UMWA, although it used a seasoned attorney, was caught unprepared for the kind of sophisticated maneuver of which Leiken was capable. The attorneys sat through a daylong hearing before an NLRB officer, which was held in the city clerk's office in St. Clairsville, a town about fifteen miles south of Cadiz and only slightly larger. Witnesses for both sides spent much of the time sitting on benches outside the city building, eating pizza and waiting to be called. The lawyers then submitted their briefs to the NLRB regional director and a waited a decision. The beauty of such legal tactics is that they are effective in damaging the union effort no matter which side prevails. Our petition to expand the Cravat voting unit was filed two weeks into the campaign, and the case took at least three weeks to resolve. That kind of delay steals momentum from a union-organizing drive, which is greatly dependent on the emotional energy of its leaders and the sense of urgency among workers. By dragging a union through the plodding legal system, we showed workers that the labor organization was sluggish and inefficient, certainly not the quick fix they might have hoped it would be.

When the sixty Cravat supervisors assembled for the inaugural meeting that sweltering day in mid -August, they could not have imagined the bloodletting yet to come. The foremen arrived under orders, having been commanded to appear at the meeting in a letter from Mike Puskarich, in which he condemned the union drive as a "crisis."

The Cravat headquarters didn't have a room large enough to fit its entire management-the Puskariches had never seen a reason to bring them all together-so the kick-off meeting was held in the basement of an aging but elegant white-steepled Presbyterian church on the outskirts of Cadiz. I got the first whiff of my prey as I drove into the church parking lot in my black Lincoln Town Car that first day. The lot was lined with aging American-made pickup trucks, each sporting a hunting rifle. Rugged men filled the church basement. They didn't know then how much time they would spend crowded around folding tables in the dingy cement hall. Twice each week, for four months, as I prepared to distribute a damning new union "fact sheet" among them, I would be calling the foremen together to make sure they understood and could promote its message.

As the men entered on that first day, most grabbed a polystyrene cup from the table in the back of the room, but not everyone filled his with the coffee cheerfully provided by Cravat executive secretaries. Rather, the cups would serve as spittoons for clumps of brown tobacco spat at regular intervals throughout the three-hour revival. A blank pad of paper and a pen sat on the table next to the cups, and next to it was a hand-lettered sign that read Please Sign Here. That was a prop, and one I had grown very proud of, for I had never seen it fail to make its point. I watched as, one by one, the men stooped to jot down their names. After signing, some sauntered to the edge of the hall and leaned against the gray wall to study the commotion before them. Others approached a circle of buddies, slapped one or two of them on the back, and exchanged tense laughter. A few seemed oblivious of the others, walking right up and claiming a folding chair, then swinging it around to straddle it like a horse. They stared at the hulking Puskarich brothers and the odd band of suited men who flanked them at the bride's table. These were mountain men. Young and old, all wore the faded flannel shirts, the hunting caps, and heavy leather boots of their trade. Their forearms and backs were massive, their hands rough, their faces ruddy and chiseled, their words few. Their mistrust ran deep. Mike Puskarich spoke first. He got right to the point. "You all know the union's after us. Well, we're gonna stop them, and here's the man who's going to help us do it. This here is our hired gun, Marty Levitt. I want all of you to listen to him. He's in charge."

I stood and launched my campaign. Except for one disclaimer at the end of the morning, I didn't alter my kick-off show for the miners. They had to hear it all, no matter how esoteric, no matter how offensive. I had to convince those mountain men of at least the injustice, if not the villainy, of the union system they had been taught to revere.

"This is no union campaign," I announced to the silent gathering. "This is a war." I liked to entertain as I taught, so I packaged my message in melodrama and comedy. From beginning to end I paced up and down the aisles, gesturing dramatically, looking straight in the miners' eyes, making them take part. I never let the energy subside. "Guess who the union's fighting? Everybody. They're fighting you. This is going to be your victory or your defeat."

I didn't have their hearts, I knew. But all eyes were on me. Not a sound was heard, save the rhythmic kersplatt of tobacco wads as they hit the rigid bottoms of the cups. "If your workers vote in the UMWA, you will have failed. A pro-union vote is proof of your inability to lead. If you let it happen, both your workers and your company will suffer-permanently." My aim was to coerce the foremen into thinking of themselves as holy warriors. Of course, the Crusades imagery worked best if the foremen truly came to believe that the union was evil and that to sabotage it was akin to doing God's work. So the miners were in need of a little reeducation.

Putting on a mock air of ignorance, I challenged, "What is a union?" I scanned the faces, blistered by the sun. Already many eyes had softened. A few volunteered definitions: workers fighting for their rights; an organization that could negotiate a contract on behalf of the workers.

Wrong, I told them.

A union was a business just like we were. And what did any business need to survive? Money. Now, it so happened that the United Mine Workers had suffered great losses over the preceding decade. The U.S. mining industry was in deep retrenchment. The sulfur-laden coal like that mined in southeastern Ohio had been blamed for acid rain. Minerals companies had closed, merged, relocated, and otherwise restructured, shedding union contracts and union member s in the process. In the preceding ten years the UMWA had lost 60 percent of its members. Partly because of declining employment and partly due to admitted financial mismanagement, the union had operated in the black only once in the preceding twelve years. The net worth of the organization had dropped in half over that time.

I turned to Mike Puskarich, who apparently was learning something new himself that day. "Mike, what would happen to Cravat Coal if you lost sixty percent of your customers?" Fortunately, his posturing didn't get in the way, and I cut him off as quickly as I could.

A business gets money from its customers, I continued, and uses the money to pay workers, buy more equipment, expand the business. By federal law a union can get money from only one place- the membership. Everyone knows that unions charge dues: that's how they pay that organizer and that attorney back in West Virginia. Bu t dues are only part of union money madness, I declared. Striking a tone of sympathy, I asked, "How many of you were aware that unions can levy fines on their membership? If a worker does something interpreted as 'anti-union'-it can be as trivial as talking against the shop steward-that worker can be sent to a union trial and made to pay a fine." When membership dwindles, as it had in the UMWA, the union starts to run out of money, I told my listeners. Sooner or later the union has to go on the warpath to colonize new groups of workers. That's what we had here-not an organizing drive, but an invasion.

"This union is desperate," I declared. "They're going to do whatever it takes to restore some of their lost revenue. That's why this is a war."

I went on, pacing energetically. I was preparing to deliver one of my favorite anti-union analogies, and I always got melodramatic when the time came. "Do you have any idea what supervising at Cravat will be like under a union?" I asked the group.

I scanned the faces and focused on a young, blond, gentle looking man: "You married?" I asked.

"Yes, sir," the man replied, his twang revealing a life in the Appalachians.

I moved in closer. "You love your wife?" "Yes, sir."

"You sleep with your wife?"

The man blushed. "Uh, yes, sir."

"Well," I continued, "how would you like it if your mother-in-law slept between you and your wife every night?"

The crowd broke out in laughter, and a voice from the back of the room hooted, "Not bad. You should see his mother-in-law." Well, maybe you're lucky, I told the boy, but most of us wouldn't want our mother-in-law in bed with us. That's what it will be like for you if we let the union in; everything you do or say to your employees will have to be cleared through the mother-in-law, the union steward.

"And who will the union steward be?" I asked. "Well, let me tell you; he'll be the laziest worker you have, the one with the biggest mouth. Union stewards don't work for nothing, you know. They get all kinds of union perks, time off for union business, super-seniority, special privileges, bonuses." That steward, I told my recruits, would be the foreman's nightmare and the nightmare of every hardworking miner on the crew.

So what could the foremen do about the union threat? It was time for a lesson in law. I walked to the back of the basement room and picked up the legal pad on which the miners had signed their names. I handed the tablet to the miner sitting nearest me and announced that everyone should make sure he had signed the paper. While the tablet was being passed up and down the aisles, I distributed copies of a federal government guide to the National Labor Relations Act. The fact that the booklet was a government publication was not serendipitous. It is crucial for the union buster to establish that what he is doing is sanctioned, even promoted to a certain extent, by the U .S. government. The labor law guide spelled out what an employer could and could not legally do to thwart a union-organizing attempt. The booklet would teach the miners the limits of the law, and I would tell them how to bend and even break those limits.

I started by outlining the four forbidden actions in an anti-union campaign. They were the fundamentals, not because I was so concerned about upholding the law, but because I wanted my trainees to learn to commit the acts without appearing to do anything illegal:

"A representative of management cannot threaten employees," I warned, "but we're going to show you how you can deliver threats without doing anything unlawful. A manager cannot interrogate employees. We'll teach you how to interrogate without asking any questions. You cannot spy on employees, but you can sure keep an eye on them, and you cannot make promises. The ban on promises is tricky. You'll see that while management is barred from promising anything, the union goes about wooing your workers by making generous promises that it can't keep."

I walked up to two miners. "Hey, you," I said in a playful one to one, knocking him gently on the arm. "At the end of the meeting this guy here's going to give you one hundred dollars. I promise." The two laughed. "Well, what do you think?" I asked the rest of the group. "Would the law allow me to make a careless promise like that?"

The miners waved their hands and booed to show they knew better. Of course not. Ah-ha. Tricked you. Suspicious looks turned inquisitive when I declared that I had just given an example of the kind of promise unions make all the time, and that they are perfectly legal. "The law forbids the party with the power to deliver from making promises," I explained. Since the company, not the union, has the power to raise wages and benefits, authorize more vacation, guarantee job security, or improve safety conditions, the company is barred from promising any such rewards during a union-organizing effort. The union, on the other hand, can promise whatever it wants, because all it is really doing is promising to ask management for something. All the union representatives are going to do is go to the company and ask for the goods it has already promised the workers.

I referred to the discussion of collective bargaining in the government booklet I had handed out. I asked a miner to read one key sentence. While the chosen young man was still struggling to pronounce the first word, I realized he was illiterate and quickly moved on to someone else. The second man read: "Neither party is required to agree to anything or to make any concessions." There you have it, I told the group. When a union wins the right to collective bargaining, it wins only the right to ask. The workers may get more. But it is also possible to wind up with the same or get less than they already have.

"Do you suppose your workers knew that when they signed those union authorization cards?" I asked the men. "I bet most of them never even read the card."

It so happened that the United Mine Workers authorization card, like that of many unions, doubled as an application for union membership. I proposed that most of the workers who signed did not realize they were applying for membership and might be angry to find out that the union had hoodwinked them into it. The workers had, in essence, signed a blank check. I picked up the yellow pad signed by all the foremen and held it up for all to see. "Did all of you sign this paper voluntarily?" I asked the crowd as I moved slowly through the room. Heads nodded. "Well, let me tell you what you signed." I began reading a lengthy mock membership authorization statement, which included the following declaration:

> We the following individuals do, of our own free will, affix our signatures to a blank sheet of paper to formally bind us to this authorization. Effective this date, we unanimously agree to pay the Marty Management Union an initiation fee of $1,000 and subsequent monthly dues of $200. We also agree to pay any special assessments or fines, which, from time to time, will be levied. We swear our oath of allegiance and fealty, over and above all other considerations, to this union and its constitution and ritual.

The idea of the gimmick was to get the word out that the workers had been buffaloed into signing the authorization cards. It was our hope that some workers would call the union to ask for their card back. They would be told that the cards were union property and would not be returned. All we needed were a few skeptics to plant the suspicion among workers that they were being railroaded by the union .The skepticism also would serve to sow the first seeds of divisiveness.

What could the company do to fight for its freedom? I asked my audience. Then I answered for them. I told the foremen the legal limits were clear: to get our message out, they could make statements of fact, or of opinion, as long as the statements did not constitute a threat. They were not to worry about what to say. We, the experts, would take control and supply them with everything they needed for the campaign. We would supply the facts, in the form of twice weekly letters signed by the general manager to be distributed by foremen to the workers. We would supply the opinion, through group meetings at which the letters would be discussed. We would supply the methodology, teaching the foremen at group meetings and at individual sessions how to approach their crewmen and track each worker's union sentiment. All we asked from foremen was the emotional commitment to beating the union. From that day until the election, nothing was more important than the anti-union campaign.

Up to that point everything in the kick-off meeting was standard operating procedure with a homespun appeal. One thing was different, however. As the meeting drew to a close, I looked out over the roomful of weary faces and offered a disclaimer. Above the objections of my colleagues, I decided to confess to the men that I understood what the United Mine Workers meant to some of them. I said I knew some would find it impossible to rally to the cause of defeating a union that had helped put bread on the family table for generations. I invited supervisors to come to my office after the meeting and discuss any problems they had with the anti-union campaign. That afternoon, as I was going over strategies, six men appeared at the door. They asked me not to force them to fight the UMWA; it would be too hard on their families. I did not let the foremen out of the campaign. They would be expected to deliver letters to their workers like everybody else and to track their men's loyalty to the company. But I had to be realistic. I knew that those men's allegiance to the UMWA would make them a threat to the anti-union effort. So I told them I did not demand the same level of commitment I expected from the other foremen. My advice to Puskarich was to work around those men and let it go. But he never forgave their treachery. Within three months after the union had lost the election, Puskarich had fired all six.

Throughout the campaign, a small, bare conference room at the converted motel served as our mission control. The room was equipped with a table, a few chairs, and a phone, nothing more. That is where, week after week, my fellow union busters and I met with foremen, questioned them about their anti-union efforts in the Cravat pits and tipples, taught them how to "work" each of our bulletins, and interrogated them about the activities of any employee we considered an effective union activist and therefore dangerous. Crosbie, Juodenas, Fisher, and I stayed in Cadiz composing letters, planning strategies, running meetings, and keeping the pressure on the Ohio foremen.

A few weeks into the program, I convinced my colleagues in Cadiz that things would go better if we all dressed in jeans and sweatshirts rather than in the business suits they preferred. Being an entertainment-oriented consultant, I always liked to dress for my audience. The way I saw it, the only way to be successful with the Cravat miners, truckers, and machinists was to look like one of them. My colleagues disagreed. Most labor relations consultants, but particularly those at Three M, like to look expensive. They figure it is easier for a client to swallow a billing rate of several thousand dollars a day if the consultants are dressed for success. Nonetheless, since my Three M companions were working at my behest, they bowed to my wishes, and by the third week all of us were dressing as if we lived in the dusty mountain town. We sent Kevin Smyth to the Kentucky mines, where he gladly dressed in blue jeans and single-handedly annihilated the union.

Once the campaign was on its way, the Puskariches stepped aside and gave us run of the company. They left the executive secretaries at our disposal and ordered all other headquarters employees to do whatever we commanded. Throughout the counter- drive we had the managers doing research and the clerical workers-whom the Puskariches liked to call their "office princesses" -typing and distributing letters, supplying us with coffee, and otherwise catering to our wishes. For our individual meetings with supervisors to be fruitful, it was necessary for us to find out everything we could not only about the foreman, but about his workers. So one of our first demands was to the personnel director. At our request she drew up a detailed diagram of company employees, listing all workers in each division under the name of their foreman. The chart included the worker's date of hire, his pay, whether or not he was married, and other details from the personnel files. Armed with that information, we immediately held the advantage over our prey. When a foreman walked into the meeting room, sometimes after driving a hundred miles from the pit where he worked, he was confronted with two cool, well- rehearsed hit men waiting to work him over. He knew very little about us, yet we continually managed to surprise him with the information we had about him and his men. We kept charts on every employee, identifying each with one of five marks: a plus sign in a circle if he was staunchly anti-union; a plain plus sign if he leaned toward management; a minus sign in a circle for a strong union supporter; a simple minus sign if he was pro-union; a question mark for unknowns. Each time we interviewed the worker's foreman, we updated the grade. We also kept notes on whatever anecdotal tidbits our informant proffered, from statements the worker had made about the company or union to details of his finances and sex life.

Each session lasted thirty minutes to an hour. Part of the time was spent on small talk and gossip, a planned informality that was meant to make the foremen feel that we were their friends and confidants. In fact, in my first meeting with each foreman, I assured him that whatever he said was confined to that room; no one else would ever see the notes I was keeping or hear the secrets he revealed. That, of course, was a bold and cruel lie. Whenever a fore- man divulged a potentially useful bit of intelligence about one of his troublesome pro-union workers, the word was passed to the Puskariches, let out on the grapevine as a damaging rumor, or filed away for use in a future strategy.

Yet the assurances got many men talking. After a few meetings with each foreman, I knew who was sleeping with whom; I was privy to the details of personal conversations among employees; and I knew many of the workers' vices, fears, and passions. One foreman was so taken by the confessional mood of the sessions that he admitted to having killed a man in a barroom fight. Even I in my cynicism was astounded to hear a man confess murder to a stranger. Yet I understood. The foreman, the front-line supervisor, has the worst job in any business-watched and hounded by upper management, mistrusted by his workers. He is alone in the middle, with no one to turn to. The supervisor's isolation and vulnerability make him the ideal tool for union-busting campaigns. The union buster shows up, and suddenly what the lowly foreman says and does really matters. I constantly reminded the Cravat fore- men that I was now their main man and warned them that a union victory could mean an end to their job and possibly an end to the company. I insisted that they were responsible for both the job security of their workers and the wellbeing of the company at large.

Despite their weakness for the intimacy of the interrogation sessions, and their fears about the future, the Cravat foremen turned out to be one of the toughest groups of supervisors I ever encountered. They resented the interview sessions from the beginning and were determined to obstruct them.

On the other side, the union's campaign was choreographed by a handful of District 6 staffers led by former miner Jim White. The group labored under the watchful eye of a higher local union official, UMWA executive board member Tony Bumbico. But White, Bumbico, and the rest of the men from the union office were not often seen at Cravat. They were not allowed; as soon as the organizing effort was uncovered, we advisers had the company tack up No Trespassing signs at every plant, pit, and tipple. That kept the union people away and forced them to do their organizing after hours. White and his men did their job; they spent evenings and weekends visiting workers' homes or meeting with them in saloons.

Meanwhile they trained nearly forty men to work the organizing from the inside.

The organizing committee is the heart and the soul of a union campaign, for they are the people. At Cravat, committee members came from throughout Puskarichland; they were miners, mechanics, machinists, and drivers. There was hardly a Cravat employee without a friend-and quite often a relative-on the committee. The committee called itself Cravat Miners for the UMWA. I called them "pushers" in a not-so-subtle allusion to street crime. They were pugnacious, they were outspoken, they were unafraid. The guys didn't hide: they included their names on the committee letterhead, and some even allowed their photographs and direct quotations to be used in a brochure enumerating the many ways in which Cravat workers were mistreated. The inside organizers did their best to keep the pro-union energy high, talking continually to workers on the job, visiting them after work, meeting them on weekends. They passed out nearly as many letters as I did, each one bearing the motto We Deserve the Best.

The foremen, for the most part, sympathized with the organizing effort of their subordinates and were stubborn in their loyalty both to the union and to their men. They submitted to the structure of the counter drive because they had no choice, and many played a skilled game of passive resistance. The foremen varied their avoidance techniques, playing dumb, lying, making up stories both about what they were saying to workers about the union and how each employee was responding. When a foreman was such a serious problem that we could make no impression on him, we referred to him as "useless" and began to work around him, assigning other, more "loyal" foremen to get to his workers.

We endeavored not to let a foreman get to that point, however. I was unforgiving of their diversion maneuvers, but it was not my style to badger, at least not a t the beginning. I was fonder of trapping an incorrigible foreman in his own deceit:

"So how's Charlie doing these days?" I asked one foreman on his regular visit one morning about a month into the campaign, referring to one of the union sympathizers on his crew. "Have you made any headway with him? What's he saying about the union?"

"Oh, Charlie's come around," the foreman lied, waving his hand as if to dismiss the thought that the worker ha d ever been a problem. "He's not union anymore. I'm sure of that."

"How do you know? What doesn't he like about the union?" "Oh, he says he doesn't want to pay all those union dues. He says it's too much money, just like the general manager's letter said."

I knew the foreman could not be trusted. He had never given me a straight answer. So, to throw him off balance I gave him an assignment. I handed him a letter detailing the UMWA's finances, including District 6 salaries and other expenditures. I told him to take the letter to Charlie and talk it over with him. I wanted to know just what Charlie thought about how the union spent their members' money, I said. Then the crucial order: The foreman was to be back in my office at two P.M. Such assignments and deadlines were part of my standard arsenal. An unwilling or unsuccessful foreman would find himself forced to confront the same pro-union workers over and over again day after day and report the conversations to me. He could keep on lying, sure, but the pressure usually got to him, and inevitably the supervisor would pass the pressure along to the wayward worker.

At the end of each week the advisory team met with the Puskariches to chart our progress, tally up the growing number of potential anti-union votes, and talk about the more troublesome supervisors.

In the end, most of the foremen did break down. They began asking their workers to vote against the union, but only when fear had overcome them- the fear of losing their job or of seeing their men or their families suffer even more than they already had. I knew foremen to approach workers and say, "Hey, I know you need this union, but please don't vote for it. If the union wins, that's the end of me. You and me a.re like brothers, and I just couldn't go on."

While my fellow advisers and I were busy making life hell for the foremen, attorney Leiken was working his magic with labor law. Five weeks into the campaign, the NLRB regional director upheld our contention that the union voting unit should be broadened to include the truckers, the farmhands, the quarry workers, and the Kentucky miners. That was good news, and a key to our ultimate victory. The expansion added about 150 souls to the roster of eligible voters, which meant more work for union organizers

We had already started working those groups in preparation for the decision. The union, on the other hand, had to scramble to find the additional workers after hours and to recruit and train employees who would run their campaign at each new site. There was more to the victory than that however. The petition and hearing process had been so encumbered and so lengthy that in pronouncing its ruling, the NLRB director also extended the usual time line for union elections. Theoretically a union election must be held within thirty days from the date the regional director calls for a vote. In the Cravat case the NLRB saw fit to triple the time, setting the election date for December 16. That gave us all the more time to discredit the union and plenty of time for any wounds we inflicted to fester.

Once a union voting unit is established and the election date is set, federal labor law requires the employer to provide the union with the names and home addresses of all eligible employees. That law, which grew out of a 1966 U.S. Supreme Court decision, was intended to give unions easier access to the employees they are attempting to organize. But a good union buster knows how to pervert the intent. When I prepared the list (called the Excelsior list, for the company Excelsior Underwear, Inc., involved in the landmark court ruling), I did so meticulously: I provided the minimum information legally required while withholding enough derails to frustrate union officers in their hunt for employees. I never included first names, for example, only the first initial. I listed the employee's house number and street, as required, but always was sure to leave out apartment numbers and street designations such as Street, Avenue, Drive, or Place. I never included zip codes. Such a skeletal list guaranteed that some employees would not be found and that the union would rake an inordinately long time finding others. To top off the sabotage, I sent a letter to every employee on the list before releasing their names to the union. In the letter, which was signed by company management, I informed employees that we had given out personal information on them to the union as required by law and assured them that we would never have given out such information otherwise. The letter went on to warn the workers to expect harassing phone calls and visits from union officials at their homes. Management apologized, of course, for the trouble the union drive was causing the good workers. I prepared Cravat's Excelsior list and warning letter according to the formula. Working in tandem with the expansion of the voting unit, the ploy was particularly effective. The union-organizing process was contaminated from the beginning.

We continued to hold mandatory meetings in the Presbyterian church basement; two mornings a week before reporting to their jobs, the foremen filed into the hall to hear a progress report on the counter union drive, received another stack of bulletins, and learned how the latest information should be presented. The first letter that I had made the foremen hand out had been a sort of introduction to the power mongering and divisiveness of unions. "Dear Fellow Employee," the letter earnestly began, as did all that followed, and it introduced the union as a self-serving outsider. In the letter we warned workers that they would be lied to and used by organizers to further the union cause. In all the letters every word was carefully planned; terms describing the union always carried derogatory and threatening connotations. We always called union leaders "bosses," for example, to repel the image of the union as a true worker organization. Meanwhile management was painted as humble, caring, righteous. Subsequent letters detailed the union's policies on dues, fees, fines, and assessments, divulged union rules and disciplinary techniques, warned that a strike would ruin the company and jeopardize jobs, and otherwise argued that the union would poison Cravat.

The other experts and I coached the foremen not to put workers on the defensive when they were following up on a letter. We warned them against approaching a worker with a question like "Did you read the latest letter?" A one-word answer would put an end to the conversation. Worse, such a question from a superior could invite a hostile response and heighten the passion of the union war. Instead we directed the foremen to point out something interesting in the letter and to make a benign comment such as "Hey, I didn't know unions could fine their members and take people to trial, did you?" or "I had no idea the United Mine Workers spent so much money."

It was not enough, of course, to cast doubt on the motives or effectiveness of the union. At a company like Cravat, where upper management was the cause and the target of the union drive, even a feeble union organization would garner support. As long as the managers in question continued their abusive and arbitrary con- duct, the union would appeal to the workers. So the second imperative of the campaign was to humanize the executives in the eyes of workers. That was a particular challenge with the Puskariches. Workers held a deep-seated hatred for the family, who seemed to think that the way they treated employees was their business and nobody else's. I convinced the Puskariches that they faced sure unionization if they continued to rule by intimidation. So, for the sake of defeating the union,

Mike Puskarich and two of his brothers, Pete and Nick, were willing to play the part of the repentant bosses. The hulking owners visited the pits and other work sires and exchanged jokes, robust laughter, and gossip with the men-in effect, tried to show they really understood their workers. The Puskariches got carried away by the showmanship of the effort and within a few weeks actually seemed to enjoy their new role. It started to look as though they really were changing. In my early union-busting days I had been convinced that an anti-union drive could bring about such changes of heart, that the threat of a union could shock an arrogant management into recognizing its failings and transforming the company. By the time of Cravat, however, I had fourteen years and nearly two hundred union busts behind me, and I had learned that was rarely the case. The Puskariches were just doing what had to be done. After the union election they became even more tyrannical than before.

While the Cravat owners were parading themselves as kind and fatherly, their sons and sons-in-law set out to befriend the miners and prove that the workers could trust the younger generation. That was a strategy I used often in fighting a union at a family- owned business. When the old-guard family members were disliked, I liked to show that changes were coming. Our humanizing effort, then, featured the new generation, displaying its members as more sympathetic than their fathers and fathers-in-law.

The younger Puskariches had a dual mission: to win the hearts of the miners and to take over the anti-union propaganda work for foremen who had proven useless. In the final weeks of the campaign I named a sort of supervisor SWAT team headed by Mike Puskarich's twenty-three-year-old son, Little Mike. The fifteen supervisors in the team, including other Puskarich family members, took charge of visiting the crews of uncooperative foremen and making sure their workers got the same heavy doses of anti-union talk and subtle threats as everybody else.

At Cravat I was lucky in that some of the younger Puskarich clan were indeed good miners and well-liked by their comrades in the pit s. Little Mike in particular was a hardworking and articulate young man, truly one of the boys. He soon became the symbol of the Cravat fight, the sign that better times were ahead. When Mike took charge of the SWAT team, crisscrossing Cravat territory to reinforce the anti-union message among the troops, our chances of winning doubled.

We continued to monitor worker allegiance through the supervisor interviews and deep into the campaign formed a Vote No Committee of pro-company employees charged with rewarding workers deemed to be "loyal" to management. Those workers found themselves showered with extra time off, special favors, and other bonuses. Meanwhile the pro-union workers came to work each day to face ever-tighter scrutiny from their bosses and were forced to battle scurrilous rumors. By that time we had established an efficient communications network capable of spreading news of perks and peril throughout the company in a day.

As the campaign progressed, the towns that dotted southeastern Ohio were ripped apart. Families and friends were divided by their union sympathies. Water towers, street signs, and billboards were spray-painted with Vote No and Vote Yes. Cravat property was vandalized. Spontaneous fistfights broke out in town and at the pits. We welcomed it all; every act was fuel for our anti-union campaign. We blamed all violence and vandalism on the union, and we endlessly admonished our foremen to point out to their crews that the union had driven a wedge of hate into a once unified work force.

The Cravat war had been raging for two months when a miner drove his pickup to a company field office and began firing bullets throughout the building. Only a few workers were witness to the rampage, but I got a phone call about the incident almost as soon as it ended, at my office in the converted motel. I immediately called for a meeting with Mike Puskarich.

The boss's reaction was as predictable as it was uncompromising: he wanted the man fired, and he wanted to prosecute. My associates agreed; they figured we could blame the rampage on the union and use the event to demonstrate the violence and savagery inspired by the UMWA. But I had another strategy.

"Look," I told them, "this man has problems. Everybody knows it. If Cravat fires him and drags him through court, the company will be seen as the villain, picking on a poor crazy guy. We don't want that. We should come forward as the benevolent, compassionate employer, show we care."

At my suggestion, Cravat had the man sent to a psychiatric clinic instead of to jail, and we spread the word that he would be offered his job back as soon as he recovered. We also made sure that any workers who heard about the incident knew that Cravat was paying the entire bill for the worker's treatment, even the portion not covered by medical insurance.

My band of experts and I mentioned the shooting incident at the next supervisors meeting. The message: The union drive had caused a great human tragedy, but the good employer was trying to do right by the man. "Here's an obvious indication of the divisiveness of the union," I told the men. "But we're taking care of him." I insisted that they tell their workers of Cravat's benevolence in the unfortunate case of Hal Lockett.

With the election about ten days away and emotions at their peak, the time came for "fun," union-busting style. I had stowed a dozen last-minute tricks up my sleeve over the years, and at Cravat I called upon my old favorites. One was the sports book: to foment a sports-like mania, I started a $1 election-week pool among the managers and foremen. Participants were to fill out an index card with their name and the number of No votes they thought we would garner. The person closest to guessing the final No vote would win $100. It was amazing to see how the pool took off and how accurate the supervisors could be with a $100 incentive. Even some of the most dogged union proponents gave away their hand and willingly predicted a resounding union defeat in order to improve their chances of collecting the prize. I used the pool as a way to get an eleventh-hour reading of workers' union sympathies while circumventing labor laws that prohibit management from conducting straw votes among employees during an organizing drive. By getting the supervisors to predict the way their workers would vote, I could test our own predictions. In pool after pool the supervisors were astonishingly accurate. Generally the median guess was only a few votes off the final tally.

As it turned out, Mike Puskarich won the Cravat pool; it was a victory char seemed to thrill him as much as winning the election. In fact, he had already pocketed his $100 prize when I shamed him into handing over the winnings to his office cleaning lady.

The miners couldn't participate in my gambling game, but there were other activities planned just for them. Corniness had become a trademark of my campaigns, although not one that was fully appreciated by my colleagues in the anti-union business. The essence of the campaign was to make it a daily event, and never was that more important than during the final days. I knew that many workers would decide how to vote in the last couple of weeks, so I wanted the words Vote No everywhere the men looked. Typically, the way I did that was through such election campaign paraphernalia as T-shirts, hats, buttons, and patches.

When I floated the idea at a strategy meeting with my fellow consultants, they objected. Juodenas was particularly strenuous in his opposition; he didn't use such gimmicks in campaigns, and he feared the T-shirt ploy would make the counter-union forces look ridiculous. My experience proved otherwise; the ubiquitous Vote No message-even if it was announced by a T-shirt-had a powerful psychological effect on the voters. Nonetheless, I agreed to launch the shirts on a trial basis: about ten days before the election. By then it was late November, and the mountain air was frosty, so rather than T-shirts I ordered five hundred thick cotton sweatshirts. In white lettering on the front and back of each navy blue jersey the words Vote No and a box bearing an X declared the anti-union cause. On the back we also printed the rallying cry "Win with Cravat." Along with the shirts I ordered Cravat Coal caps and Vote No patches.

I gave a shirt and hat to three foremen and sent them out to the largest work sites. Within a few hours they came back with orders for dozens more. It seemed everybody wanted them. At the next meeting I handed out the shirts and hats to all foremen, who took the goodies to their eager crews. Two executive secretaries, Dottie and Kitten, became so intoxicated with the carnival atmosphere of those final days that they sewed anti-union patches onto strategic, suggestive spots on their blouses and slacks.

I knew that many of the workers wearing the shirts, hats, and patches were not against the union. In fact, some of the most aggressive pro-union people ordered the shirts as cover for their sentiments. Many others wanted the shirts just because they were free. It didn't matter. The net effect was that the anti-union message enjoyed a high profile in the week before the election.

Behind the scenes, the campaign was anything but frivolous. Ed Juodenas made up oversize copies of the plus-and -minus charts we had been keeping on the workers and papered the walls of our conference room with the humongous loyalty report cards. It was a dramatic military touch that had us calling the conference room our "war room" from then on. Any worker still classified as a question mark was being reported on practically by the hour, and we kept our Magic Markers handy so we could log the continual updates on our battle charts.

With a few days left before the vote, Cravat got a call from an NLRB election agent. The NLRB had designated twenty-six polling places throughout the Ohio Appalachians and Kentucky, and some of the nine board agents were afraid to drive their government cars along the winding, icy roads of those isolated mountain territories. Their concerns left us an entree to make a pass at the NLRB. We told the agents we would gladly drive them to the polling sites- many of which were out at the pits-in company four-wheel-drive wagons. When the union activists heard about our plan, they were outraged and demanded that a union election observer be allowed to ride alongside the polling agent. We, of course, refused, threatening to take back our offer if union people were ordered along. The NLRB denied the union demand. So on election morning, several polling agents boarded Cravat trucks and headed for the polling sites in the company of a Cravat driver. That was one more victory for us: in a union - busting campaign, the relentless accumulation of small victories leads to the final big win.

By the time the balloting was under way, I had no doubt that the election was ours. Mike Puskarich was equally sure and even hand-delivered his $71,000 final payment to me before the election results were in, an unusual move among union-buster clients. The fight cost Cravat a tidy $250,000, not counting attorney's fees. My portion of the cake exceeded $60,000.

(Editor's note: $590,000 plus attorney's fees in 2014 dollars)

White, Bumbico, and the UMWA were equally certain of a union victory-so sure, in fact, that top UMWA officers showed up to watch the ballot counting. The UMWA happened to be holding its international convention in Pittsburgh at the time of the election, and Richard Trumka, the young, charismatic international president of the union, took a day trip to Cadiz to observe the election. In light of the latter-day losses of the UMWA, the Cravat vote was expected to mark a turning point for the union. My fellow consultants and I stayed away from the ballot counting, which took place at a machine shop in Cadiz. We sat, from 4 A.M. election morning until night, in the comfort and protection of the executive offices. Telephones rang constantly as Cravat managers called to give us continual updates. The tension didn't break all day.

By 10 P.M. it was over. The final count was in, a chapter in Cravat history ended. With 391 workers casting ballots, the union won only 93 votes. The remaining 298 were ours. The Puskariches, company loyalists, and we advisers spent the night in drunken celebration at the Holiday Inn in nearby Steubenville as the union mourned.

Bumbico was devastated by the loss. He told the Wheeling Intelligencer newspaper following the election that Cravat workers had lied to the UMWA about wanting a union. The next week Bumbico sent an angry and sneering letter to Cravat employees. In it he reproached the miners for their lack of resolve and rebuked those who had signed UMWA cards and then voted against the union. Bumbico accused the workers of having used the United Mine Workers to push for the improvements they wanted, without any intention of forming a union. And he predicted, rightly, that Cravat management would never change. In closing, Bumbico vowed to never take on Cravat Coal again: "You and your Company [can] have your second chance. But there is one thing we can tell you as a certainty: if things don't work out -WE WILL NOT COME TO YOUR AID TWELVE (12) MONTHS FROM NOW....

Two years later, in the middle of a four-year term as a regional director for United Mine Workers, Bumbico left union work and took a position as human resources manager with Central Ohio Coal, a private coal company.

Consider the past year.

Have you seen examples like the ones in this chapter?

Blatant examples, like:

- Constantly portraying the Union in a bad light?

- Dividing the employees into groups and then pitting them against each other with different policies or bonuses?

- Promised confidentiality that was just words, like surveys?

- Trying to humanize senior management to the employees, using pictures with kids, pets, etc?

- Seen different treatment for 'pro-company' people?

A page from the Editor

World Airways is a classic case.

Look for some of the techniques that are not central to the theme of the chapter. For instance, can you find where pilots are fired from World and then re-hired by a subsidiary to reduce the number of union pilots?

And how delaying every interaction with the Union was used to wear them down? Every grievance was taken to arbitration. No matter the cost.

And the 'Dear Fellow Employee' letters that are used throughout union busting. How many have you received?

A short comment by an NJASAP member can be heard by scanning the QR code below.

It's all about control, and this story mirrors the many tactics used to divide and conquer in our situation.

The Editor

MembersSpeak®

Scan the code to listen or go to
http://bit.ly/1pLA7gn

World Airways

When I met Edward J. Daly in November 1973, he was not widely known. Eighteen months later, however, on April 3, 1975, Ed Daly grabbed international headlines when his Oakland-based charter airlines company, World Airways, completed a wildcat evacuation of fifty-eight orphans from Vietnam. Newspapers had been following the story for weeks, chronicling the exploits of a gruff ex-boxer from Chicago's south side—multimillionaire, international business tycoon, daredevil adventurer, and theatrical sentimentalist. The news hounds wanted to be there—and Daly wanted them there—when he pulled off his most spectacular display of philanthropy. They had followed Daly to Danang, where he was clawed bloody, wounded in the stomach and head, and nearly killed as he and his crew fought amid machine-gun fire and exploding grenades to rescue Vietnamese children from the blood-letting that followed the American pullout from Vietnam. They related how he slugged South Vietnamese soldiers who were pushing aside women and children trying to board the plane, and how he strained for two hours to hold closed the rear door of the damaged 727 during the flight to Saigon. The news people followed him on to Saigon, where from his suite at the Caravelle Hotel he tussled with the South Vietnamese government, the U.S. embassy, Secretary of State Henry Kissinger, and even President Ford over the political urgencies of the on-again, off-again plan to save the children. Daly reportedly launched that famed first flight in defiance of Saigon airport tower officials. Newspapers covered the story lustily. They carried wire photos of the pugnacious, thick-faced Daly, sporting his trademark green beret and safari suit and displaying a heavily bandaged right arm, at a Saigon news conference where he announced the rebel flight. When the jet landed at Oakland International Airport a day later, the news people were there. Accompanying lengthy and dramatic accounts of the mercy mission were black-and-white photographs of crying children and sweet young women, of somber-looking pilots, of crowds gathered around the hull of a World Airways jet waiting to greet the most defenseless victims of the war in Southeast Asia. The next day the Oakland Tribune quoted an angry Ed Daly rebuking President Ford and Henry Kissinger for having ignored warnings that a massacre of refugees in South Vietnam and Cambodia was imminent. "I didn't even get the courtesy of an answer to my cables," Daly protested to the Tribune. That was Ed Daly.

At the time of Daly's airlift, newspapers also carried another, decidedly more lighthearted World Airways story. In the restrained prose of business journalism, newspapers reported World's proposal to offer regular $89 flights between the East and West coasts. The drastic cut in coast-to-coast airfares, from the typical price of $194, was a bold move in those years, when fares and routes were tightly regulated. That, too, was Ed Daly. Over the previous decade World Airways had become a household word throughout the country as the largest charter airline in the world. By the early 1970s 21,000 travelers a year gladly boarded World's crowded DC-8s for a bargain-priced journey to Europe, Asia, and the Middle East. They willingly tolerated the discomfort—the jets had been reconfigured to fit additional seats—for the chance to fly across the world for a fraction of the regular ticket price. The newly proposed scheduled service was, for Daly, a characteristically bold move and a unique challenge to the major airlines. As it turned out, the service would not be approved for six more years, during which time Daly tussled with federal regulators over volumes of objections lodged by the major airlines and watched his business descend into insurmountable debt.

When he dared to dive into competition with the likes of TWA, United Airlines, and American Airlines, Daly was known in the industry as the irreverent chief of a most unusual airline company. Daly was an outsider—simultaneously respected and resented by many of the more conventional airline executives. He was impetuous, unpredictable, and utterly arrogant; now abundantly generous, now shamefully tight. The same paternalistic boss who personally paid medical bills for the children of needy employees was also a raving maniac who once demoted a stewardess on his private plane for forgetting to replenish the A-1 sauce. Daly was severely alcoholic; when he died of kidney failure in 1984 at the age of sixty-one, friends said he looked at least twenty years older. Working or dealing with Daly was a complicated affair, and he inspired intense and conflicting emotions in those around him. They revered him; they despised him. He would not be told what to do; the only rules he followed were those proclaimed by him, and even then he would consider himself exempt. Do as much as imply to Ed Daly that there was a rule or a convention that bound him, and he would find the most spectacular, most destructive, and often most humiliating way of breaking it. The rules he hated most were those imposed on him by labor unions.

When I read Daly's name in the Herb Caen column, I didn't know a thing about World Airways, new as I was to the Bay Area. But I found out that, to Oakland, anyway, the company was a big deal. It was the Oakland Airport's leases to World that, more than anything else, gave the upcoming airport a chance at the big leagues. In 1973 World ran four major operations: the commercial charter business, a $60-million-a-year enterprise that made World the largest charter airline on earth; military airlifts under contract to the Department of Defense; aircraft leasing, with clients the likes of Jordan's King Hussein and the Republic of Yemen; and aircraft maintenance. In 1973 World had signed a forty-year lease with the Port of Oakland, which administers the airport, for a mammoth $14 million jet maintenance complex built for World by the port and the federal government. The maintenance facility soon became one of the Bay Area's largest business centers, employing two thousand workers within a two-hundred-thousand-square-foot hangar on a sixty-acre site at the entrance to the airport's general aviation field. In addition, World filled a large hangar deep within the airport compound, which served as corporate offices, and leased a terminal gate for commercial charter flights, by far the largest component of World Airways business at the time. World was traded publicly, listed both on the New York and Pacific stock exchanges, but really the company belonged to Ed Daly. The one-time pugilist and ex-GI built World from the ashes of a two-year-old debt-ridden cargo airline that he bought in 1950 for $50,000—legend has it that he made the purchase with winnings from poker games aboard a troop ship during World War II. Until his death, Daly owned 80 percent of the stock.

World was a high-profile airline, owing to its ultrahigh-profile chairman. The company always seemed to be cooking up some daring business feat, taking on impossible foes, and confronting insurmountable odds. And it seemed always to be winning. But that image was somewhat distorted. "World was an insignificant airline, really," says David Mendelsohn, former deputy to Chairman Daly. "[But] Ed was a firm believer and a great practitioner of creating the image he wanted to create. His way of giving [the company] life, weight, was for him to appear bigger than life. It was his way of getting the airlines in the paper. The media focused on him as chairman, as a personality, and gave him the PR he wanted."

Despite its grand public face, by the time I was introduced to the company World Airways was already in trouble. Twelve long years before the company shut down everything but its minuscule leasing business, laid off thousands of workers, and pulled out of Oakland, the seeds of financial disaster were spreading their roots. In 1973 World Airways made a profit of just over $1 million, peanuts, really, considering the company's revenues that year were almost ten times as much. The company lost nearly $11 million on its four core businesses, only partly because of the oil crisis that year and resulting rise in fuel costs. The only way World managed to show a profit for 1973 was from the sale of a California bank, First Western Bank & Trust, which World (read Daly) had purchased in 1968. As with the rest of America, the year 1968 had been a pivotal one for World Airways. It is no coincidence that 1968 and 1969 were peak financial years at World Airways: the United States was at the height of its military involvement in Vietnam, and World was bringing in more than $50 million a year— accounting for more than one-third its annual revenues—in military contracts for cargo and passenger airlift services between the United States and overseas bases. By 1970 World's military contracts dropped almost to half, and they didn't recover until near the end of the decade, interestingly, after the Iran hostage taking.

Hidden within World's 1973 financial report was the essence of Daly's entrepreneurial forte: deal making. The charter business, although it grew to be huge and was considered the backbone of the company, never did make money for World, Mendelsohn said. In fact, World rarely made money on its continuing operations. But Daly had a Midas touch when it came to deals; buying and selling were his gifts. Ever since 1955, when he bought a fire-gutted DC-4 for $75,000, renovated it, flew it for five years, and still made a $100,000 profit off its sale, it was clear that Daly was a born negotiator. "That's what Daly did best," Mendelsohn said. Woe to those who sat across the bargaining table from him.

It was no secret that Daly longed to take on the major commercial airlines, to show them, by God. His foray into scheduled air service was proof that his dream of being one of the big boys was as constant as it was sincere. In a slap at his weighty competitors, Daly's newspaper advertising campaign promoting the scheduled service pictured World Airways as the biblical David slinging stones at the airline industry's Goliath. Nonetheless, the cowboy executive never sacrificed his other businesses to that ultimate ambition, for the leasing, airlift, and charter businesses afforded Daly an entree into global affairs. Through his international business, both military and commercial, Edward J. Daly was able to play a part on a larger world stage and participate in major global events. In addition to his role during the Vietnam War, through World Airways Daly insinuated himself into the Hadj, the annual pilgrimage of Moslems to Mecca, providing charter service to the holy city; invested in Jordanian hotel resorts; and helped set up airlines in Jordan, Yemen, Mali, and South Korea. Daly was constantly on the prowl for other international deals as well and was forever flying off to the South Pacific or the Far East or Africa to confer with some powerful foreign head of state. According to Daly lore, the World Airways chieftain would drink and haggle over price for hours with kings and presidents, then settle the dispute with an arm-wrestling competition. Daly always won. His first mate knew why: "He would cheat," Mendelsohn says with a wink.

Despite Daly's lust for bartering, the ultimate deal he might strike was almost beside the point. The around-the-world sojourns played a more meaningful and much more complex role in the life and psychology of an impossibly complex human being: Daly's internationalism made him big and important and powerful. Often he put his greatness to work on behalf of the very meek. Daly never managed to establish the Samoan airlines he longed for, for example, but his perpetual dialogue with the Samoan government led to a close relationship between him and the highest-ranking Catholic clergyman in the islands. A proud and resolute Irish Catholic, Daly ended up donating a great deal of money over the years to the church projects and even financed the education of six Samoan students at the University of California at Davis. As compulsive in his charity as he was in other arenas of his life and work, Daly's benevolence sometimes took the form of highly publicized acts of philanthropic bravado, as in the Vietnam airlift. Other times his generosity was silent and sweet. Daly was known to pass out $100 bills to the diminutive residents of Bay Area orphanages every Christmas. He wrote out countless checks to nuns for their pet charities and made continuous donations to the University of Santa Clara, a Jesuit college near San Jose, where he sat on the board of regents and board of trustees for two decades.

Although Daly's paternalism inspired loyalty and love in many, it also bred resentment. Paternalism works only as long as the recipients are willing to be treated like children and to maintain a posture of gratitude and humility. People might well go along with it, I suppose, as long as their needs are being met. But among World Airways office workers, that was just not so. Pay was low; benefits were almost nonexistent. The core of the problem, however, was Daly himself. His blustering and rash behavior, intensified by heavy drinking, made Edward J. Daly a very troublesome boss.

I started calling Daly's office as soon as I read about him in the Herb Caen column. I called for ten days solid. I talked to the receptionist, to the executive secretary, and to Daly's personal assistant. I insisted, I warned, I cajoled. Daly wouldn't bite. Later in my career I would come to pride myself on my ability to reach the chief executive, no matter how expert their secretarial screens. Others in my field would come to envy the way I schmoozed and bamboozled my way into executive suites, while they were stuck bickering with weary secretaries in the outer office. Daly was a different breed, however. The executive ego was nothing new to me, and I knew well how to kiss it, massage it, and threaten it to get what I wanted. But Daly was not just another schmuck executive; he was a king. Truly. A meeting with Daly was referred to as an "audience." When he wasn't globetrotting, Daly kept himself locked in a lavish, ballroom-size suite furnished with antique inlaid tables, Chinese vases, Persian rugs, stone sculptures, and other treasures. There, accompanied by his Pinch Scotch and Russian vodka, which he poured into a large Baccarat crystal glass, Daly remained insulated from the prosaic with the help of three layers of offices and a contingent of vice-presidents, assistants, and secretaries. The ladies and gentlemen of the Daly court were expected to protect His Majesty from intrusions, fielding all pleas for charity, handling daily business matters, and doing away with pests like me. After the hundreds of sales calls I made over two decades, Daly remained the only chief executive who never came to the phone.

It took me two days just to get my phone calls to World routed into the executive offices. Finally my message of urgency made its way to David Mendelsohn, which was as far as it was going to go. When Mendelsohn called me back, he told me plainly, "You'll have to deal with me." Even he wasn't going to make it easy. His calendar was full. He would meet with me in two weeks.

Well, damned if I was going to let this fish get away, not with an idyllic home and a gorgeous new girlfriend waiting to make my California dream come true. I was working another campaign at the time—in Michigan, of course—and I saw World as my way out of that deadly air commute. I shot back at Mendelsohn, "You're wasting precious time, you know. Time is critical here. Every day you leave this thing unattended you're giving the union momentum and strength. There's no one who can better handle this than the man you're talking to right now. You're a damn fool if you let it get out of control. Will you be around tomorrow?"

Dave wasn't budging. He answered opaquely, "I'll be in the office, but I'm booked up all day."
I started thinking about Alice, about all we could do together if I were in town more, about all we could have if I proved my worth to Three M and won a fat raise. Hell, if I could sell myself to John Sheridan and Herb

Melnick, I could sell myself to Ed Daly. But I had to get to him first. The next day I drove my pumpkin orange Volvo station wagon out to the Oakland Airport and found my way to hangar six, home of the World Airways corporate offices.

I knew I would not be readily received, and I was prepared to camp out at the World offices all day. I ate a big breakfast and brought along a full pack of Winston cigarettes—the only non-union brand at the time—and my trusty nail clipper. I always kept my clipper in my pocket. I clicked away with it in the way Nick Sangalis used to clack worry beads, fiddling with it sometimes for hours to relieve tension and boredom.

At the receptionist's area outside the executive offices on the second floor, I told the young woman behind the desk that I was there to see Dave Mendelsohn. She warned me that since I had no appointment she didn't know when he could see me. I assured her I would wait as long as I had to and took a seat on a small sofa. There I sat, quietly reading magazines, smoking, and fidgeting with my nail clipper. Occasionally I smiled at the receptionist, but otherwise I kept to myself, seemingly undisturbed by the wait. After about an hour and a half the receptionist picked up the telephone receiver in response to a buzz, looked over at me, then whispered, "Yes, he is." A few minutes later, out stepped Mendelsohn.

Dave Mendelsohn wasn't really an airline executive. He was really a banker, and that's just what he seemed. He outfitted his six-foot frame in traditional blue or gray suits, carried himself upright, moved deliberately, and spoke sparingly, generally without a trace of emotion. He was a serious man and a brilliant accountant, whose cold circumspection provided a crucial counterbalance to the raging genius of his boss. As a senior vice-president at Bank of America, Mendelsohn had been Daly's banker for four years. When, at age forty, Mendelsohn was offered a promotion at B of A that was to take him away from Daly's accounts, the World monarch made him a counteroffer. The way Mendelsohn tells it, "Daly said, 'Come with me and write your own ticket.' Banks paid terribly then, so I accepted." Mendelsohn took over a tiny office not far from Ed's and toiled for the next three years to keep the lid on Daly and World's bottom line in the black. Mendelsohn shared the responsibility of Daly damage control with half a dozen other men who guarded the corporate inner sanctum. Their titles and official duties varied, but their job was essentially to pamper Daly and cater to his every wish, but somehow to keep him from destroying his company and himself.

It was an impossible task. Daly refused to delegate or in any way relinquish control, insisting on making all decisions himself. Yet if he wasn't off on a transcontinental jaunt, he was usually drunk and in no condition to be deciding how to spend money or whether or not to fire somebody. The titles bestowed on some of World's top officers reveal the autocratic nature of Daly's leadership. The title of vice-president and director went to Daly's wife, Violet June. After her, assistants abounded: there was Mendelsohn, vice-president and deputy to the president and chairman of the board; there was Charles Patterson, vice-president and assistant to the president and chairman of the board; there was James Cummins, vice-president and personal assistant to the president and chairman of the board. Below them came Michel Rousselin, chief administrative assistant to the president and chairman of the board. Even those with less complicated titles, like senior vice-president Brian Cooke, were called upon regularly to serve as Daly's attendants and messenger boys.

"Daly made everyone become his personal valet," says Michel Rousselin, who worked for Daly from 1970 to 1980. He told of a time when Daly had Cooke open a door for him, then compelled his senior vice-president to remain in the doorway for five minutes so that the door wouldn't slam shut. Daly expected such indulgences, Rousselin says. He craved attention, and image was all-important: "That's why he wanted flunkies like me standing around all the time."

Just months before I arrived, Daly's manic control had driven the president of the company to quit in disgust. Howell Estes, a dear old friend of Daly's, had been recruited just two years before, but it didn't take the newcomer long to understand that his presidency was a sham. Estes was no lightweight army buddy. He was a retired four-star air force general, tough, bright, and accustomed to being in charge. That was the trouble. There was no room in Daly's world even for a second-in-command. Estes had no authority; he was just another member of the emperor's court. After Estes quit, Daly appropriated the title of president, abandoning the more bureaucratic designation of chief executive officer.

Under Daly's crazed and explosive command, World's spending was chaotic and sometimes ill advised, and employees—including top executives such as Mendelsohn—were constantly being fired for no apparent reason, sometimes only to be rehired as soon as Daly sobered up. Yet many loved working for Ed Daly; he made life interesting. If he wasn't throwing a fit or a party in the office, he was stirring up gossip on some far corner of the earth. It was exciting even to be an accounting clerk for such a brash soul, to watch him storm through the building, to be picked by him for some small personal task, to whisper about his latest tirade, to hear the tales of his personal abandon. Also, as fiercely as Daly punished impertinence, he rewarded loyalty. He knew most employees by name; they could count on his help with their personal troubles. If Daly got wind that some hardworking employee had suffered a family tragedy, he might send flowers, but it would be accompanied by a check for $5,000. During the Christmas season, it was not unusual for Daly to fill his pockets with a few thousand dollars in cash and take a stroll through the office, doling out the money along the way.

What made Daly fascinating, however, also made him treacherous. The sudden and rash firings were no secret, and office employees knew they worked at Daly's whim. "He ran the company with fear," says Curt Steffen, World's vice-president of labor relations during the 1970s. Of World's 3,000 employees in 1973, 2,500 were already union and therefore somewhat protected from the uncertainties of Daly life. The mechanics, drivers, pilots, and cabin crews who made up the bulk of the World work force were represented by a nearby Teamsters local. Only the white-collar employees were still not organized, and Daly was loath to let them fall. He resented having to deal with the Teamsters and spent a great deal of time and money over the years just to make the union's job tiresome and difficult. If the Teamsters wouldn't go away and leave him alone, then he would make them slug and grunt for every inch. For example, whenever a union member filed a grievance against the company, he challenged it on principle and steadfastly refused to settle the difference, Steffen says. Daly insisted that Steffen take each and every complaint through the full, months-long grievance process, all the way to the last step, arbitration. The company spent thousands of dollars along the way, and so did the union. Steffen said he personally fought more than one hundred grievances on behalf of World, and lost only two. Daly also spent hundreds of thousands of dollars during the mid-1970s to prevent the white-collar workers from unionizing; the Teamsters tried twice to bring the clerical workers under the union's wing. Daly tried to oust the Teamsters altogether during a string of labor strikes and work stoppages from 1975 to 1977. Although he never succeeded in ejecting the Teamsters, Daly did become quite adept over the years at weakening the union's grasp. Former employees tell how, by laying off workers from World Airways and having them hired by his foreign airlines, Daly was able to remove a number of pilots and flight attendants from the union contract. The fact that Daly kept Air Mali and Air Yemen employees out of the union riled the Teamsters and was a continual bone of contention during contract talks. But Daly was intransigent. He said simply but emphatically that those were separate companies, and they were non-union.

Daly's anti-unionism was virulent. Perhaps that is because "it was less a business philosophy than a personal battle," as Michel Rousselin says. "No one [told] Daly what to do. He was a one-man band, and no one was to stand in his way." Lest the battle lines be unclear, Daly designed a workplace motto to inspire and guide his troops. As clerks and mechanics labored, they could look upward and receive their Daly counsel. On the wall above them hung the admonition: "Perfection, not correction." Indeed, there was one voice at World, and there was never any question whose it was.

My first meeting with Mendelsohn went well; he was intrigued by my spiel about utilizing the supervisors and clearly entertained by my zeal. He wasn't going to give in easily, however, knowing it would be up to him to build the case to Ed Daly: "What you say makes sense, but we already have good representation in these matters." Mendelsohn told me World had an industrial relations man, Steffen, whose full-time job was to deal with labor issues. On legal questions the company turned to Gibson, Dunn and Crutcher, the Los Angeles-based mega-law firm that has represented numerous celebrities, including Ronald Reagan during his presidency. My presence, it seemed, would be superfluous. Yet Mendelsohn was charmed enough by my youthful gutsiness that he agreed to talk it over with the attorneys. Before leaving his office, I was sure to get the lawyers' names. I knew I needed them on my side if I was going to get this job. I planned to give them a call myself.

With Gibson, Dunn and Crutcher, World was in very capable hands indeed. The airline's lead labor lawyer, Jerry Byrne, was an expert in the Railway Labor Act, the 1926 law that, together with its 1934 amendments, still defines worker-management relations in the railroad and airline industries. His partner, Steve Tallent, also was well schooled and intelligent. It would be a pleasure working with such a top-notch pair, if only I could get their blessing. I reached Byrne by phone at his Los Angeles office and launched my pitch, mixing my practiced tone of certainty with just the right amount of deference for Byrne's superior knowledge and his seniority: I wouldn't presume to tell him how best to do his job, oh no. I wanted only to offer the services of my company for the technical tasks.

"As a labor attorney you already know that the best way to get to the workers is through their supervisors," I teased. "Now, I'm certain you don't want to go in and do all that work with supervisors. Well, that's what we do. We run the campaign at the company level and let the attorneys concentrate on the law." Byrne thought he had heard of Three M, but he was skeptical. Labor law could be tricky, and he didn't want to risk letting World fall into legal trouble because the consultants had been clumsy. It just didn't seem smart to hand over control. Now, the last thing I wanted was for an attorney to feel he was being shoved aside. So I promised Byrne, "We won't pass gas unless we clear it with you. Even though we're planning the campaign, you have the last word. If there's an emergency and we have to get a letter out right away, I'll call you and read it to you. There won't be any surprises." I always kept my word, too. Not only did it keep me just out of reach of the law, but it fed the attorneys' piggy banks, and they always remembered that. I needed attorneys to get work, and there was no faster way to get the lawyers in my corner than to make money for them. Every time I called an attorney to clear a letter, it was another fifty dollars on his meter. They loved it.

Byrne said he would be in Oakland in two days and agreed to meet with me then. In the meantime he talked to Mendelsohn and set up a conference at World headquarters. There, I was to meet one more member of the World inner circle—Brian Cooke, Daly's somber, even-tempered senior vice-president, who was to assume the presidency after the emperor's death. After letting me talk for a while, Byrne quizzed me on my knowledge of the Railway Labor Act. True to form, I hadn't even bothered to look at the railway act before going into my meeting. But Tom Crosbie had warned me that the question might come up and had supplied me with the official Three M bluff: "If they ask you, tell them you haven't worked under it, but that there are principals in the firm who are very expert at it," he told me. Three M liked to sell itself as a highly evolved company, with a methodology so developed and a staff so highly trained that the consultants could be considered "interchangeable parts." A client need never worry that we might not be able to handle a situation.

The Railway Labor Act would be no problem; I had been briefed enough on it to know that it is even more generous to employers than the National Labor Relations Act, because it does not specify what employers may and may not do to combat a union-organizing attempt. The National Mediation Board, which oversees union elections for railroads and airlines, does not involve itself in the organizing process to the extent that the NLRB does. There are few ground rules and no list of unfair labor practices for union election campaigns. If a union feels an employer has broken the law, its only recourse is to sue in federal court, which of course is very time consuming and costly and holds to higher standards of proof. That gives railroad and airline companies an even greater advantage over unions than other employers, who at least have to contend with the nuisance of responding to unfair labor practice complaints.

Crosbie had told me, however, that attorneys wouldn't want to hear how we would take advantage of the law. They would just want to know that we wouldn't cause them any headaches. So I delivered my lines as instructed: "I'm not the expert, but from what I know, we would still conduct the campaign as if it were under the National Labor Relations Act." So we would be law abiding. Byrne liked that.

The World executives and their attorneys endorsed my campaign strategy. It made sense: if we wanted the office workers to turn down the union, we had to convince them that Daly was willing, indeed eager, to change the way he ran the company. In order to do that, we had first to convince their supervisors, who felt more directly oppressed by Daly than their subordinates. But the kid-glove approach would be so out of character for Daly. How were they going to sell him on it? Mendelsohn, Cooke, and the attorneys said they needed to talk it over, then they'd ask for an audience. Would I please wait outside?

I returned to my perch in the reception area and resumed smoking and clipping. Time dragged on. I was uncharacteristically nervous, too nervous to read or chat or smile or do anything but wait. As the minutes ticked by I began to feel vaguely sick. My stomach was upset, and I was dizzy. The anticipation of this Daly character had gotten to me. Finally Mendelsohn emerged: "Mr. Daly will see you."

Oh, God.

Before Mendelsohn and I were allowed to enter Daly's chambers, Michel, Daly's personal assistant, checked my appearance. He then led us through his office to the solid wood door that stood as the final separation between Daly and the commonplace. Michel knocked lightly, then opened the door, holding it in the manner of a butler as we entered. When I saw what lay beyond the door, I almost rubbed my eyes. Before me stretched a great room, so filled with treasures that I felt I was entering a sacred museum. The suite was sixty feet long and at least thirty feet wide; everywhere there were hand-woven rugs, Oriental screens, marble statues, and porcelain vases. Daly sat at the far end of the room, behind a heavy antique desk. The entire suite was darkened except for a pair of white lights positioned on the high ceiling directly above the desk, which illuminated Daly like a holy shrine.

Mendelsohn and I approached slowly, silently, with the reverence of worshipers entering a great cathedral—or perhaps the throne room of Oz. As I walked I half expected to hear a thundering voice intone: "I am Daly, the Great and Terrible. Who are you?" I knew instinctively that I should not be Marty the Small and Meek. Powerful men rarely respect submissiveness, even if they demand it. I would play Daly the way I had played other corporate chieftains—only much more so.

The great and terrible Ed Daly looked oddly out of place amid his ornate surroundings. A broad, rugged-looking man with a bulbous nose, he seemed more suited to the corner bar. But, of course, Daly didn't have to go to the corner. On the top of his desk, shimmering in the spotlights, stood a tall crystal glass filled with an amber liquid. The air around him was thick with the pungent smell of Pinch Scotch. Daly was half-drunk and feisty.

"So you're the fella who thinks he can help us get rid of this union bullshit," he boomed. "Why should I hire you?"

I was ready for the pissing contest. "I don't think you have any choice, Ed," I said coolly. "From what I've heard, this union's gonna kick your ass."

He knew it, too, and he launched into the most profane tirade against unions I ever heard, before or since. When he recovered, we got down to business. I explained how my program worked and forewarned him that he would be called upon to humble himself, just for a while, if the strategy was going to work. He would have to tell his troops that he knew he had made mistakes and convince them that he wanted to change. He hated the idea of playing the softie. He was a fighter; he wanted to make war, not love. Ed Daly was not about to do any sweet-talking. Most of the bosses I worked with felt the same: here they were, all primed for rape, and I come around and start talking seduction. But then I explained how it worked, how we wouldn't hold back, we would just make department managers and supervisors do it for us. Then the cruel smiles appeared. That was even better. Let them rape each other.

Daly relished the maliciousness of the plan as much as the rest of them. He wasn't too happy with the nice-guy approach, but the strategy intrigued him. He was going for it. "I hear you're expensive," Daly said with a snort.

"You get what you pay for, Ed," I shot back. As a junior member of the firm, my fees were then $350 a day. I was going to be working with two more senior consultants, who charged $500 a day. I couldn't say how much the whole thing would cost; that depended on how long it took.

Daly didn't like uncertainties. He didn't mind spending money, and lots of it, to slaughter the union, but he wanted control over how much. "Do the whole thing for twenty thousand and you're hired," he pronounced.

I jumped for it. I had been with Three M only a few months, and surely didn't have the authority to sell a job at a discount. As it turned out, the voting didn't take place until July 1974, seven months later. The final bill would have been more than twice Daly's offer. But I was afraid to let Daly get away, so I made the deal. I was to catch hell for it later from Melnick.

On the job with me were Tom Crosbie, whom I had called constantly during my courtship with World, and Jim Bannon. We set up shop in Howell Estes's old office, which had remained vacant since the general's resignation, and also made use of the ornate corporate boardroom. Bannon and Crosbie both were based out of town, and they juggled the World campaign with others they were running simultaneously. As the West Coast partner, Crosbie also was responsible for coordinating a dozen other consultants. He hopscotched around the country Sheridan style, looking in on campaigns and collecting fat fees for his presence. For Crosbie, World Airways came in handy as yet another base of operations for Three M's itinerant business. When he was present he spent much of the time holed up in the president's office, phoning clients and associates, hunting down work, and helping out with other campaigns in progress. I was on the World job more consistently than the others and therefore handled the bulk of the one-on-ones and the letter writing and was the designated emissary to Daly's office. But the dynamics among the three of us were crucial to our drama. Each had a specific role to play, with a script written to suit his character. We played off one another masterfully.

Bannon was the numbers man. He could churn out anti-union statistics like no one else. From union leaders' salaries to the potential cost of a strike, Bannon could combine the numbers so that they told only the story we wanted workers to hear. Crosbie played bad cop. He was expert at it; he knew how to be mean and to make his meanness effective. From a white-hot rage he could suddenly turn cold as ice, frightening reluctant supervisors into obedience. I got the part of good cop, my favorite. As

Crosbie beat away at the managers, I romanced them. I was their refuge from his cruelty. They turned to me for protection, and I became their priest and their pimp. I heard their confession, counseled them, then sent them out to sell our lies to their friends.

We launched the World campaign with a flurry of activity, as we always did, cranking out two or three letters a week and calling in the supervisors for propaganda rallies each time. Daly didn't involve himself, except to sign the letters and hear a weekly progress report. Daly gleefully signed any letters that ridiculed the union. If the tone was even vaguely conciliatory, he was less willing and had to be cajoled. Occasionally Daly was too drunk even to read the letter. Then we would take the circular to Michel, who had become quite expert at forging Daly's signature. It was just as well that Daly stayed away from the campaign. It would be a lot easier to do a makeover on him if he remained out of view. At the group meetings we stuck to our roles: Bannon filled the crowd with facts, Crosbie intimidated, and I made love.

"Remember the Golden Rule at World," I told my captives time and time again. "We're family." We divided the supervisors among us for the private meetings, then cross-checked each other continually. We had learned that although some supervisors would be able to deceive one of us, virtually no one would be adept enough to trick all three consistently.

Since we were dealing with office workers, most of the supervisors were women. Generally women were more easily intimidated than men and also more eager to believe in the possibility of change. But the World Airways ladies were a tough bunch. Anyone with a few years of Ed Daly behind her was sure to have developed a hard edge and a thick layer of skepticism. They were even more mistreated than their subordinates, and they dumped their complaints on me in the interviews: "We need something that can protect us from Ed Daly"; "Look what Daly did to Wanda—that could happen to any of us"; "He gives us a ton of responsibility and no authority"; "You never know what he's going to do when he's drunk."

Daly was a loose cannon, they knew. They told me how every few months he'd turn up in the large, open, office area and go on a rampage. Like a trigger-happy sniper, he would survey the office inhabitants, looking for a target. Anything could set him off: a cluttered desk, a little casual chatter, an unbecoming outfit or hairdo. He'd zero in on his prey and fire. Towering over the victim's desk, he would curse and pound his fists, shouting insults like "Get off your butt, you lazy slob. What are we paying you for?" or

"What makes you think you can work here looking like that? Go comb your hair." Often he would drive the poor woman to tears.

Daly was not always so terrible, but he always kept the pressure on. Supervisors despised his meddling into the day-to-day affairs of their departments. He kept his fingers on all the controls yet still held them accountable for every detail. So tight was his hold that department heads could not even give their employees time off to go to the doctor or to a funeral without his written approval. The invisible thumb of Daly was pressing on them all the time, even when things were quiet. Many supervisors told me privately that they would organize a union for themselves if they could figure out how to do it; they would have loved to have a contract. They seemed quite unconcerned about the possible consequences of their private blasphemies. Like the rank-and-file employees, the management people had learned not to waste time wondering how Ed Daly would react. He'd do what he'd do, and not even he would know what it would be until the last second. There wasn't a thing anyone could do about it.

Perhaps no one knew that better than Michel. Michel's formal title was chief administrative assistant, but that oblique designation belied his intensely intimate relationship with Ed Daly. Michel was a genteel, dignified man, one who dressed impeccably in European suits and spoke with a refined French accent. He occupied the office just outside the chief executive's and thus was the final buffer between Daly and the irritations of the outside world. Daly compelled all his executives and assistants to serve as attendants and whipping boys; it was not uncommon for him to phone Mendelsohn or Brian Cooke or Michel at two in the morning to harangue them about a misdeed or demand some immediate service. But no one carried a more personal burden than Michel. Michel cared for Daly's drunken body, battled his angry spirit, and endured his humiliations more than any of the others. Michel poured the drinks, drove the limo, did the shopping, fetched the coffee, carried the luggage, and listened and listened and listened. From 1970 to 1980 Michel was the companion Daly loved, then reviled, then loved again. He was fired and rehired at least six times during those years.

Michel was not at all of one mind about unions. He felt the Teamsters behaved horridly, for one thing, and he didn't know what to make of their antics. But he did know Daly. "He was an animal, very primitive," Michel says. "Ed Daly was a genius: he could sit with a pack of lawyers and outwit them all. It was instinctive. But he was terrible with personal relations. He hurt people terribly, over and over again." He also was very stingy. Michel calls World wages "just adequate." Employees received minimal medical coverage and enjoyed no pension plan.

Clearly the job of convincing Daly's employees that they didn't need a union was going to be tough. Taming Daly would be impossible, we knew. We would have to try to keep him on a tether until the voting was done; he was going to be a big, big problem. From the beginning, we had another problem. It, too, had a name: Curt Steffen.

Curt, a veteran union organizer, former airline executive, had been working as World's labor relations hit man since the year before Three M arrived. Just weeks after Curt was hired in 1972, Daly had bumped the former personnel director out of his office and installed Curt, with the title of vice-president. From that moment until 1977, Curt worked as a one-man front line in Daly's never-ending battle with the unions, slugging it out with the Teamsters day after day. He did Daly's bidding in the tedious war over grievances and executed His Majesty's orders to fire or demote or punish employees as suited each particular transgression. Curt was tough, and he was loyal. A stocky, muscular man with a permanent scowl and a smoldering temper, he was perfect for the role of union antagonist. Curt had started his labor career much like Sheridan, as a staff member and eventually president of an IBEW local in Chicago. He went on to become an organizer and negotiator with the Airline Pilots Association and later landed a job as the vice-president for labor relations at Universal Airlines in Chicago. Then, somehow, word got to Daly that Curt Steffen was looking for a job. Daly knew of Curt and had been looking for a toughie to help him keep the unions humble; he made Curt an offer. There was no time to think. Daly had told him, "Get here on Monday." Curt took the job.

Thanks to Ed Daly, Curt was on the rise. He was the resident expert in labor matters at a daring airline and was forever talking in the president's ear, telling him how to handle this or running to get his approval for that. Over the past year Curt had come to consider World employee relations his personal fiefdom, and he guarded his domain jealously. Then along came Three M, and suddenly Curt Steffen was irrelevant. He was not invited into the anti-union campaign. In fact, he was shoved aside. Curt was expected, like everybody else, simply to show up .at our meetings and do as he was told.

From the first day it was clear that Curt meant to cause us trouble. It enraged him the way we came in, took over his job, and started bossing people around. Here he was, up to his elbows in Daly's dirty work every day, and suddenly he wasn't good enough to shovel the real shit. Who were we, anyway? Three soft-skinned boys in fancy suits walk in and suddenly everybody has to sit up straight. Well, he sure as hell wasn't going to. He had been doing just fine without us. Daly cherished him, wasn't that so? It was Curt, after all, who had prepared Daly's f-word letter to union organizer Louis Celaya, which I had read in the Chronicle.

Ironically, Curt objected to Daly's stubborn refusal to let the clerical workers organize. Not that Curt was a softie. Hardly. But he was pragmatic. He had worked for and with unions for many years, and he knew how to handle them. He used to tell Daly that it was much easier to control employees when they were organized. With a union, everything was institutionalized. There was a proper way to ask for something and a proper way to complain. It was all spelled out.

"I used to tell him, 'With a union, I only have to deal with the business agent. It's better to have five business agents come to see me every day than all these employees with all their complaints,'" Steffen recalls. But Daly wouldn't have it. He wouldn't let go.

Now, just a month after the Celaya letter, Curt couldn't believe what was happening. Suddenly he found himself sitting with the other World executives before an audience of sixty supervisors at the kick-off meeting of an anti-union drive in which he would have no say. There he was, shoulder to shoulder with a dozen other officers of World Airways, in a manufactured show of management solidarity against the union. He stared out at the faces of the department heads and supervisors who filled the giant classroom. Before him, Tom Crosbie and Marty Levitt and Jim Bannon were prancing and dancing around the room, shaking their rattles and playing their war drums. And all he was supposed to do was listen and nod. It made him sick to his stomach.

Curt did listen, enough to know he hated every damn word we said and enough to know he was going to do what he could to work against us. When that first dog-and-pony show ended, Crosbie, Bannon, and I approached Curt to let him know what we would be needing from his office. We were going to want the names of all supervisors and the employees who reported to them, as well as all pertinent personnel information on each one. We talked to him dispassionately, as if giving an order to a waitress in a fast-food restaurant. Curt puffed his chest and stuck out his chin.

"Okay, you guys are here now. There's nothing I can do about that," he grunted. "But this kind of shit I can handle myself." With his whole body shaking, he barked a summary of his background— excluding the felony.

Crosbie responded coldly: "Okay, so you're the personnel man. Congratulations. Just understand one thing: we're running the show."

When Curt had left, Crosbie called Jim and me to a powwow. "This guy, he's not going to play ball with us. Watch out for him," he warned. "Don't give him too much. We may throw him a bone every now and then, but that's all. If he can do something to make us look bad, he will. Don't give him anything he can use." We were used to having to contend with wounded personnel directors, and generally it didn't bother us. We had learned that most executives saw personnel work as merely clerical—the administration of payroll, benefits programs, and the like—and that they generally resented spending money on it. Many of the companies that hired us, even relatively large ones, did not even have personnel departments. They saved their pennies by distributing the various tasks among the secretaries. Where there was an actual department designated as personnel or, more contemporarily, human resources, more often than not the function continued to be mostly bureaucratic. The human resources officers screened applications, put together the policy handbook, handed down judgments on leaves of absence, and produced tons and tons of employee-related paperwork. Personnel directors were just midlevel administrators, not leaders. I came to expect that the head of personnel would be the most incommunicative and unempathetic bureaucrat in the plant, possessing little vision and no authority. Rather than seeing human resources as a vital support service for employees—as the name suggests— our clients tended to consider the whole department a costly bother. As a result, we were able to completely overrun the personnel office, taking charge of the employees and appropriating even the most closely guarded information. The director might have grunted and groaned, but the way his boss figured it, it was about time the damn department was put to some use.

Curt Steffen was a little more problematic than most personnel chiefs. He whined plenty about our stepping on his toes, but our conflict with him turned out to be weightier than the usual battle over turf. Curt's objections to us were substantial, and he worked hard throughout the campaign to sabotage our strategy. Those people did need a union, and he knew it. So there he was, talking at Daly, telling him the workers would never swallow the bullshit we were churning out; there he was again, cursing our names and speculating on our high prices; and over there, ridiculing our message of love and our promises of change. Perhaps, had Curt been another type of man, he would have won. Perhaps, had he been able to harness his rage and suppress his pride, Curt would have been able to undermine us as he hoped. But Curt was a visceral being, one driven by passion and incapable of the self-control required to carry out a protracted war with an ice cold enemy. He was easy to provoke and not hard to disable, given the right weapon. Against Curt, our weapon was indifference. We didn't let him engage us in battle. We dismissed him, brushed him aside.

As exciting as it was to be working for Ed Daly, the real focus of my life was Alice. I thought about her day and night and spent much of my day hiding out in my office at World composing love letters or calling her on the phone. When Alice was working, I left messages for her at hotels in Boston, New York, Washington, St. Louis. When she was home, I was useless. I was so eager to be with her that I could hardly think straight. I knew she would be waiting for me, so I cut out of the office as early as I could and sped to fetch her from her parents' home. I romanced her the only way I knew how, by spending a great deal of money. We ate at expensive restaurants; I bought her fancy jewelry and sent her elaborate bouquets. We spent our nights together at Holly Road, drinking exotic liquors, bathing in the hot tub, and luxuriating in the peace and comfort of that Marin hideaway. Alice and I planned to marry in April 1974. With the wedding just a month away, we rented a small house in the charming bayside town of Tiburon, just down the hill from the Holly Road house, and began making plans for a honeymoon in Tahiti. The World Airways union vote was set for July, so the schedule seemed perfect.

It wasn't—not to Ed Daly, anyway. One night, around midnight, the phone rang. It was Dave Mendelsohn. I had been blabbing about my impending nuptials for weeks, so certainly the wedding was no secret, nor were my honeymoon plans. Those plans were the problem. Daly was getting nervous about the union drive, Mendelsohn told me; he couldn't have me so far away during the final stage of the campaign. What if the union did something sneaky? What if something went wrong? I had served as the emissary to Daly throughout the campaign, and he came to count on me as his window and his voice to the employees. He was very upset. Rather than honeymooning on a tropical island, would I consider using his cabin at Lake Tahoe?

It wasn't what I had in mind, but I agreed. I had been told that King Hussein had once stayed there, so I figured it couldn't be too bad. Alice and

I were married amid the rococo elegance of Grace Cathedral atop San Francisco's legendary Nob Hill. That night, as husband and wife, we drove to Dollar Point in Lake Tahoe, in search of Mr. Daly's little cabin in the woods. What we found instead was a grand, six-thousand-square-foot mansion that rose up like a castle on a hill high above the lake. We arrived to find the cupboards packed with full liquor bottles, the refrigerator stuffed with fine food, and the beds all dressed in satin sheets.

Life was quite different for Edie Withington and her staff at Local 29. By 7 a.m. each weekday, half a dozen of the local's most earnest men and women had deployed themselves at the various entrances to the World Airways office buildings. Wrapped in heavy sweaters against the morning fog, they handed fliers to secretaries and file clerks as they hurried to work. The union folks then headed for their own jobs, only to return to the World offices at quitting time, when they would spend an hour or two trying to talk to the workers. Edie's nights belonged to the Travelodge, one of a dozen motor inns that populated the ugly, mile-long stretch of Hegenberger Road linking the Nimitz Freeway to the Oakland Airport. There, in a stark meeting room, she would listen to World Airways office workers' troubles and try to convince them that Local 29 could make a difference. More often than not there were five or six anti-union employees at those meetings, workers who had been sent by me to disrupt the caucus and put the union on the defensive. Sometimes a couple of supervisors even showed up, a move strictly verboten by the National Labor Relations Act as an act of surveillance. But at World we were working with the railway act, and the chances of anybody making a stink about a couple of management types showing their faces at a union meeting were pretty remote. The anti-union workers made the going very tough for Edie and the rest of them. Sometimes they would shout and sneer. Other times they would ask questions—hostile, misleading questions. And sometimes they would just sit quietly, glaring at the participants and jotting down mysterious notes on little pieces of paper. Whatever tack they took, they always unnerved the employees, even if they didn't rattle the union officers. Every time they asked a question, they dropped a bit of distorted information.

"They insisted that joining the union meant you had to go on strike," Edie says. "They harped on union dues a lot. Then they said things like 'Figures don't lie, but liars figure.' It put a damper on the discussion, that's for sure."

The management plant is a standard presence at union-organizing meetings. Their job is manifold: disrupt the meeting so the union can't talk strategy; take the focus off workplace problems by turning the questions on the union; intimidate union sympathizers; report back to the management. Of course, if the anti-union workers are acting as spies, the railway act makes that patently illegal, but big deal. It's almost impossible to prove.

Edie Withington believed in her union. As a secretary at a Construction Laborers Union local and a union member for more than thirty years, she knew how unions worked and what they could do for people. She had seen lots of organizing drives and heard thousands of workers tell stories of injustice and abuse. So when she met with World Airways employees, she wasn't surprised to hear workers accuse their supervisors of favoritism, inconsistency, and a general lack of fairness. She knew those to be the capital sins of management, the corporate inequities that most often led workers to seek a union. Edie was surprised, however, at the depth of mistrust of World management and at the charges leveled against the chairman of the board himself.

"Daly scared people," she remembered, "particularly when he was drunk. Some thought he might even get violent. They had no job security. Management was arbitrary, capricious. They could get fired for anything or for nothing." Under those conditions, why weren't workers terrified of being identified with a union campaign? As Edie saw it, "They had nothing to lose."

Secondary to the issue of job security was the question of pay. In 1970 Fortune magazine listed Ed Daly among the twenty-five richest men in the world. Yet office workers at his company earned about 20 percent less than they would elsewhere, according to Curt Steffen, and their benefits package was meager. One former secretary remembers making $451 a month in 1974, which comes to about $2.62 an hour. The secretary liked her job in spite of the wages, saying her co-workers were like family. It was more than familial warmth, however, that convinced most workers to put up with World's paltry pay. For many, terrible wages were the tradeoff for the company's considerable travel benefits. Even though World was just a supplemental airline, the company made available to all employees the enviable Interline Pass, the airline industry's premier perk. With the pass and the price of sales tax, World employees could fly their families anywhere in the world on any airline. World also allowed its employees to fly for free on any World Airways plane that was being delivered for charter service. If the company needed to send a DC-10 to Paris the following month for a European charter tour, for example, employees would be invited to sign up for a free trip. So dearly did employees prize World's travel benefits that the perk became a major obstacle to the union drive and a primary weapon for us. World employees didn't have much to lose to a union fight, except the travel package. So we warned the supervisors, "You know, there's no way Ed's going to let you keep your travel benefits if the union gets in." In our letters to the rank and file, the threat was more indirect; we preached that in contract negotiations the union would have to barter for every penny and every benefit, even the ones that workers already enjoyed. The message was clear.

The World Airways administrative supervisors were an angry bunch; it was a struggle to get them to campaign against the union. To better control the battle, we set our sights on eight key supervisors, who together oversaw more than two hundred clerical workers, almost half the voting unit. For those eight we prepared an intensified version of the campaign, with double doses of everything. We mixed sweet talk with warnings and saturated them daily, starting out soft and letting the tension build, until the threat of discharge seemed the only logical conclusion. "Can't you see what the union is doing to this company?" we teased. "We were like family. Now look. What's wrong? Don't your people trust you? What have you done to bring on this union thing? Well, you'd better find out. Go out there and talk to your people and get them to trust you again. (Pause) Of course, Daly isn't going to stand for having a union in here; you know that. If you can't control your own people, he's going to hold you responsible. What you tell me in these conferences is confidential, but I am under an obligation to report your effectiveness to my client."

We demanded that the eight, as managers of key departments, turn every single voter against the union. No exceptions. We didn't want stray sheep, and we didn't want unknowns. Everybody. And if they, the supervisors, couldn't convince their own workers to have faith in management, then they would have to answer to Ed Daly. Directly. He wasn't likely to be too understanding, either. On the other hand, Daly always rewarded loyalty, didn't he? Surely he would remember someone who worked so diligently on his behalf, perhaps with a promotion—or even a raise. Even later in the campaign, when we were letting less significant supervisors slide a little, we never loosened our grip on the target eight. Each was called in several times a day and asked for an accounting of every worker in his department. Each had to fulfill several assignments daily that brought him face to face with some of the toughest, sharpest pro-union workers in the office, over and over again. After a few months the routine had the supervisors begging for their jobs, not to Ed Daly or to us, but to the pro-union workers who seemed to hold their bosses' future in their hands.

After a few weeks it was clear that threats alone were not going to be enough, particularly with supervisors outside the eight-person bull's-eye. It had been mainly my job, both at the mass communions and in our private sessions, to give the supervisors hope that Daly was willing to change—to let go a little, to delegate a little, to be a little kinder, to fix some things. Some bought into the ruse, vowing to work against the union if we could extract certain pledges from Daly. But we needed more. We had convinced Daly he could sell the employees on a program of the benevolent father, and the employees weren't buying it. So we sharpened the other edge of the sword: having lured the supervisors into the confessional, we began to use their disclosures against them and their crews. Nothing made Daly fly into a rage more quickly than a suspected betrayal. He was lord, and he expected complete devotion from his subjects. When we began reporting employees' sins, the result was a wave of reprisals that pushed the infidels into a lonely corner. In a witch-hunt, witches are always in great supply. Likewise, at World in 1974, traitors abounded. Disloyalty could be anything: a gripe, a snide remark, a little cheating with the time clock, a mistake, whatever we could use to raise Daly's ire and put pressure on a troublemaker. We tried to keep the source of the leaks secret, so that our captives would continue to feed us information. Still, people became wary.

"Marty had a reputation around the place," says Charles Patterson, one of Daly's vice-presidents. "People started saying, 'Look out for Marty. Watch what you say to him.' "

Curt Steffen got fired, sort of, for something he once said to me. He never forgot how it happened: "[Marty] would use anything you said against Daly. The interviews were tricky. They were setups. He'd lead you down this negative path, with things like 'Ed isn't always fair.' Then [you'd] say something, too, and he'd report it."

What Curt actually did was call Daly "a prick." I tattled. It gave me great pleasure. Curt had been a pain in the ass for months, and now maybe I could shut him up. Daly was drunk when I divulged what Curt thought of him; he fired Curt that same day. As often happened with Daly, however, by the next morning the transgression was forgotten. Curt was in his office piling his belongings into boxes when he got a phone call from the president's suite. "What are you doing down there?" a now sober Ed Daly demanded. "I need you up here." Curt was back on the job.

Once the campaign had settled into a routine, Crosbie, Bannon, and I found we had a lot of time on our hands. Some days we would lounge in our office for hours at a time and take turns making phone calls around the country. I called Alice, my parents, my friend Michael Krasny, or anyone else who could help me pass the time. Sometimes I found it frustrating, sitting there in a big fancy office with nothing to do. When Crosbie got on the horn to do his telephonic rain dances, I smoked and listened and clipped my nails. I was bored. After a couple of months we knew who was on our side and who wasn't, and we didn't need to interview every last supervisor every day anymore. The phone calls entertained us for a while; when we tired of that, Crosbie and I killed time talking about the Oakland Raiders or evaluating women. Eventually even those conversations ceased to be interesting, and it was time to get back to work. Crosbie would stand up, stretch noisily, and meander over to the door.

"Hey, it's pretty quiet out in the hallway. Maybe we should get someone in here. Who should we call?"

"What about Judy?" I suggested. "We haven't seen her for a while, and she's got great legs."

With the help of the in-house directory we had snatched from Curt Steffen's office, we summoned the person we had selected for the next hour's entertainment. A lot of the time the supervisors were grateful to be called. Those who were willingly carrying out our game plan saw our office as a haven from the work floor and a break from their routine. We engaged them in conversation, offered them cigarettes, swapped jokes, and used up a lot of time. One of our favorite comrades at World was the director of maintenance, a young hunk named Tom Ripa. Ripa looked like the actor Tom Selleck in his prime, muscles head to toe, a head full of black curly hair, a thick mustache, and a perpetual grin. He was our good buddy, our fraternity brother, a beer-drinking party boy with a hearty laugh. Great at guy talk. As maintenance director, Ripa supervised two hundred workers, but only six were clerical people. So, technically, he did not promise to be a key player in our campaign. But we liked Tom Ripa, and in the end he would come to play a role as important as it was bizarre.

At World Airways we never got to enjoy the cockiness that comes with a sure bet; this race belonged to Ed Daly, and he was constantly changing the odds. Still, about halfway through the campaign a company win began to look like a possibility. We had taken all the supervisors through the same basic program as the key eight; even with considerably less intensity, we had managed to convince them all that their jobs were in jeopardy should the union win. Sufficiently worried, the supervisors kept the pressure on their workers and after a few months managed to turn the campaign in our favor. We learned that the company-as-family argument appealed to many at World, so we never let up on the message of renewal. Meanwhile we had managed to keep the union on the defensive, forcing organizers to rewrite their game plan continually in order to respond to our moves and answer the questions we planted. Often, their answers were lacking. At their worst, they attacked Daly. That was the union's gravest error. So powerful was Daly's magnetism that even those who claimed to despise him yearned for his approval and worshiped him secretly. To criticize Daly was blasphemy. It was a cruel irony: the campaign was all about Daly, yet the union didn't dare mention him.

After a series of miscalculations, Local 29 was looking clumsy and ineffective and desperate. At long last workers were losing interest and faith in the union; by our estimates, the company was leading by a handful of votes. In an NLRB election we might have felt somewhat secure. Our plan would have been to keep the warmth and love in focus until the last ballot was counted, then collect our check and walk away. But a Railway Labor Act election is done differently, and it wasn't going to be so easy.

Under the railway act, a union election is conducted by mail. Voters have two weeks to mark their ballots and return them to the National Mediation Board. That two-week time lag could be a problem anywhere, but at World it practically guaranteed a union win. There was no telling what Daly might do. He was live ammunition. We could go into the election with a solid majority, only to have it demolished by one rash Dalyism.

To make matters worse, on a railway act ballot there is no place to vote against the union. If an employee favors representation, he marks the box next to the union's name. If opposed, he simply does not return the ballot. We feared that in the peace and quiet of their own homes, with time to think it over, World employees might be inclined to follow the bias of the ballot and give the union their vote. The mediation board only has to receive a majority of ballots for the election to be valid, so Local 29 could win even if almost half the clerical workers threw their ballots away in disgust, assuming that those who did mail theirs in voted in favor of the union.

With just four weeks to go before we would turn the employees loose with their ballots, our side fell apart. Twice in the final stretch Daly mounted his notorious office raids, winning a few more for the other side with each savage incursion. But he saved his most stupid display for the end, just fourteen days before the election. At that crucial moment Daly apparently found himself overwhelmed by the urge to fire somebody. So he did. It might not have mattered if he had axed an irritating supervisor or picked on one of his executives, as he had so many times before. But, as if purposely trying to foil our operation, this time he chose a sweet, unassuming, newly hired young accounting clerk, someone guaranteed to inspire sympathy among the very workers who soon would be deciding whether or not they wanted a union. The reason for the firing made Daly's deed even more outrageous: the clerk paid a bill on time. That's right. World had a rule—unwritten, as far as I knew—that no bill was to be paid until the final day it was due. If an invoice called for payment within thirty days, the check was to be issued on the twenty-ninth day. Surely the new clerk had been taught the dogma, but for reasons unknown, she paid one bill on the twenty-third day of a thirty-day contract. Daly was merciless. Then, just in case his severity wasn't being given enough attention, the tyrant dashed off a lengthy, scathing memo berating the accounting staff and warning the others not to make a similar mistake.

We didn't know if we could rescue Daly's image from his latest blunders. What we did know was that we had only one hope: His Highness was going to have to ask his subjects' forgiveness. Crosbie and I knew our next visit to Daly's suite would not be pleasant, and we wanted to be prepared; we shut ourselves in our office and plotted. Together we drafted a letter of contrition that we saw as Daly's only chance to salvage the election. The letter was to be sent by Daly directly to the employees' homes, rather than being handed out in the office, in order to create an aura of intimacy, as in the confessional. We hoped a show of humility by Daly at that moment might be enough to rekindle the hope sparked by all the promises of the past months. The threats, we knew, would not be forgotten. We were loath to ask Daly to bend his knees even a little, but we also knew there was no other way. With the trepidation of apprentice exorcists about to meet the devil, we put a call in to Daly's office to say we were coming.

Daly could not have suspected the weight of the impending meeting; we had popped in three or four times a week for seven months in pursuit of his signature. By now it was all very matter-of-fact. This time would be different, though. This time we would fight. This time Daly would howl. Crosbie pulled out the letter and handed it to Daly, who was seated—as usual—behind his desk with his glass of Scotch. The two of us remained standing, like soldiers awaiting a reprimand. Daly read:

Dear Fellow Employee,

I have taken the liberty of writing you at your home because of the extreme importance of my subject.

For many months we have all had to endure the intrusion and annoyance of an outside third party. It has not been easy for anybody. But by now you have learned that the union can guarantee you nothing except that it will take money from you and perhaps take you out on strike. Your company is not perfect. No company is. We have made our share of mistakes in the past, and we may again in the future. But nothing can justify the damage that would be caused if we were infected by an outside agent. We will accomplish a lot more through a direct relationship than an arm's length one. And so I am asking you, from my heart: Please, give us a chance. Thank you for allowing me into your home with this most important message.

Yours truly, Ed Daly.

As his eyes marched down the page, Daly's habitual scowl grew more pronounced. When he reached the middle of the letter, his face reddened. His cheeks quivered. Then he began to grunt. Finally he exploded. He slammed his fist on the desk and pushed himself to his feet, leaning toward us with rage. "What the hell are you thinking, walking in here with this crap?" he howled, throwing the letter on the floor. "I'm not going to sign that fucking shit. Get the hell out of here."

Crosbie and I were ready. "I don't think you have much of a choice, Ed," I told him coolly. "This letter is our only hope. Your people are angry. If you don't want them voting for the union, you have to make them believe that you recognize your mistakes." Then the clincher, the threat I always delivered when executives balked at playing humble: "Without this letter, I can't guarantee you the election."

In a reversal of our usual roles, Crosbie tried to be conciliatory, offering to change words here and there. But Daly would not be calmed. He ranted and fumed for nearly an hour. Then, finally, Crosbie struck gold; he came up with the only line that could freeze Daly's rage and transform it into glee. If we would add that one golden sentence, Daly said, he would sign.

He even laughed as he penned his name. In the final edition, Daly's admission of imperfection was followed by the proclamation: "As you know, I never have and I never will bow to a gun at my head." Very John Wayne. Very Ed Daly. The letters were printed on Daly's personal stationery and put in the mail that night.

Within a few days supervisors began reporting that the "Give us a chance" letter was getting a warm reception. People really wanted to believe in one big happy World family, and they wanted to believe in Ed Daly. They also wanted not to see him angry again for a while. Things were going to be all right after all, they said with a collective sigh. Well, let's face it, he has been under a lot of stress lately. He really does care; I mean, Gawd, look what he did for the people in Baja after the hurricane, and look how he helped Helen out when her husband was in the hospital. Yeah.

Crosbie, Bannon, and I knew that the renewed romance with Daly was ephemeral; and we knew we had to concoct some gimmick that would short-circuit the railway act election system. We definitely didn't want those ballots sitting on people's coffee tables for two weeks, reminding them of World's problems. We were going to have to entice employees to rip them up. The election was a long shot, but not impossible: the two hundred clerks who worked under our eight target supervisors were crumbling under the pressure, as their bosses harangued, coaxed, and begged them to declare themselves against the union. Dozens of others were openly upset with Local 29's attacks on Daly and convinced by our benevolent father routine. That put the election within reach. Now we had to come up with a lure provocative enough to induce people to destroy their ballots. But what?

We happened to be tossing around ideas after a supervisors meeting one morning when Tom Ripa joined us. He was entertained by the problem and joked about it in his engagingly macho way. With a broad grin, Ripa quipped, "How 'bout if I let my girls know that if they bring me their ballots I'll streak the airport?" We all laughed. Just imagine: hundreds of young women forfeiting their union ballots for a chance to see a hunk like Ripa running stark naked across the airport. What a scream.

No one was more surprised than Ripa when I called him into my office a short while later to say I was taking his offer seriously.

"You gotta be kidding!" he gasped. "It was only a joke."

Well, why not? I said. The mood was right. The employees had received the "Give us a chance" letter just a few days earlier and were still feeling forgiving. Half the workers were ready to nix the union anyway. The rest would be relieved by the change of pace, maybe even relieved enough to "give us a chance." Local 29 had lost its footing; maybe Ripa's heinie would be enough to push it over the edge. We called an emergency supervisors meeting and got the word out. Hear ye, hear ye: If more than half your employees rip up their ballots and turn them in to Tom Ripa before the voting deadline, Ripa will treat them to a show they'll never forget. To wit: a run in the buff. Well, the supervisors baited the hook with zeal. It was their only way out. So drained, so beaten down were my captives by then, that they would do anything to get this campaign off their backs. Grateful to finally have a product to sell, the supervisors hawked the promise of Ripa's body—and of a happy reunited company—like carnival barkers on commission. They goaded their weary subordinates: Step right up, folks. This is our chance to be friends again, to bury our differences. We need some excitement around here anyway, don't you agree? You're gonna love this.

To my surprise and delight, the workers swallowed the bait with gusto. Clerks and secretaries giggled as they egged and prodded each other. The pressure was off, finally. Throughout World Airways offices the sense of relief was palpable. Like magic, the hostility had dissolved. Seemed like old times again, workers whispered to one another, like before this union thing. World Airways was just one big family out for a little fun.

Eager to get it over with, girls and women hurried home to their mailboxes; nearly four hundred of them tore up their ballots and trotted them over to Ripa's office. And so it was that in the final days the World campaign was transformed into a circus. And so it was that we completely befuddled the men and women at Local 29, who stood by helplessly as the crowds abandoned the center ring for a silly sideshow.

We delivered Ripa as promised. Wrapped in a black fur coat and nothing else, Ripa was driven to a general aviation runway that lay in plain view of hangar six. At the foot of the airstrip Ripa disembarked, shed the coat, and ran.

What parallels can you draw from this chapter to our situation?

Have you seen or heard of pilots brought in for unwritten rules, for new interpretations that were never announced?

Experienced the company fighting every grievance, no matter how obvious they were in the wrong?

Have you ever been pushed to fly an aircraft that was questionably safe?

Seen people at Union meetings that claim they are not in management but seem to question everything the Union does?

Seen examples of former union negotiators now operating in management?

The Author Speaks®

Listen to the author of "A Union Buster Confesses", Martin J Levitt, as he speaks in his own words.

How much do companies spend a day to break a union?

Can a Union Buster break a Union without breaking the law?

Were you hired as a Union Buster or was some doublespeak used to cover your true purpose?

What is happening when management takes on a Union?

How important is it to stay focused?

In the 18 years you busted unions, how many were you directly or indirectly involved in?

Why would the Company constantly delay?

How long will Company tactics last?

How does Management use the media against us?

How much does this have to do with the CEO?

Why don't we have a contract already?

Is this all about profit or is there another motive?

What role does 'employee relations' play?

What are the tools a Union buster uses?

There are a lot of coincidences. Is this planned out?

How important is staying united and focused?

Is the Company threatened by our solidarity?

It's easy to lose focus. Will that hurt us?

Are promises of new aircraft part of the game?

The Company is treating us like every other employee. Is this unusual?

Are threats of shutting down the company common, too?

What does management get by delaying the contract?

What should we expect to happen during this time?

A page from the Editor

This chapter details the struggles of organization. Why is that important in our effort?

Because the same tricks used here have been observed in our everyday interactions with the company.

-slight changes of the rules designed only to make life more difficult.

-interpretations that have never been accepted are now forced upon us

-blaming the Union for everything.

-using other employees or outsiders to put pressure

-constantly barraging non-union employees with stories that are untrue, misinterpreted, or outright lies.

Can you find equivalent examples as you read?

The Editor

PS. Can you identify this tactic of claiming separate entities- then combining them, solely for the purpose of busting a union? Think of the fractional consolidation…

MembersSpeak®

Scan the code to listen or go to
http://bit.ly/WMV4B7

Copeland Oaks

Petition

Name of Employer: Copeland Oaks, Inc., Sebring, Ohio
Type of Establishment: Retirement home
Employer Representative: Claude L. Roe, executive director
Petitioner: Service, Hospital, Nursing Home & Public Employees
Union, Local 47, Cleveland, Ohio, affiliated with Service
Employees International Union, AFL-CIO
Union Representative: James Horton

Jim Horton entered the world in the midst of the Great Depression. As the third of sixteen children born to a black Alabama coal miner and his wife, and as their eldest son, Horton learned about work early. He also learned about unions. Horton was in grade school in the 1940s, and his papa was in the UMWA. The United Mine Workers of America, historically one of the most militant unions in the country, was roaring and growing under the raging leadership of John L. Lewis. Once a month, more often when there was trouble, the elder Horton awakened Jim at dawn and dragged him from their rural cottage to the early morning union meetings in Birmingham. Jim learned a great deal from watching his father; he grew up thinking of union men as hardworking and serious. And he grew up believing in loyalty.

At age seventeen Jim left home. His parents had enough mouths to feed, and it was high time. He said good-bye to Alabama still clutching the dream that he might one day play major league baseball. But soon after he arrived in Cleveland Jim's boyhood fantasy dissolved, overshadowed by more pressing matters, like the need for food. He took whatever jobs he could find, first at a chemical company and later with the B&O Railroad, and then he joined the Air Force.

Jim's discharge from military service four years later brought with it the GI Bill and the promise of higher education. But first things first: he had to make his way once again in the civilian work world. In 1959 Jim Horton was hired as an orderly in the psychiatric ward at St. Luke's Hospital, a stately Methodist institution in downtown Cleveland. Jim was just twenty-five years old, and the pay of $1.30 an hour didn't seem so bad, not at first. He was industrious, bright, capable. He wouldn't be staying long.

He started taking classes at the Ohio School of Broadcasting and at the Arma Lee Barber College as well; he planned to have a real career someday. But six years later Jim was still at St. Luke's, making just a few cents an hour more than when he'd started. In 1962 Jim had married, and within a few years he had fathered a son and a daughter. He started looking around the hospital. What he saw disturbed him: hundreds of workers, most of them blacks and other minorities, toiled for years at heavy, dirty, emotionally draining jobs for rock-bottom pay. The workers were frightened and distrustful, even of one another. They had no protection from the disciplinary whims of their erratic supervisors, no job guarantees, little hope for promotions, and no hope at all of one day earning a living wage. The more Jim saw, the more he wanted to know, so he started poking around, asking questions. And the more he heard, the more determined he became that something had to change. Jim found janitors and nurse's aides with ten, fifteen years at the hospital who still made well under two dollars an hour. He found a capricious wage structure that totally disregarded experience and seniority. He found long entrenched work rules that discouraged groups of employees from gathering. And he found a system of selective threats and promises that encouraged employees to compete with one another rather than to cooperate. That's when he decided to do something.

Jim couldn't know that his call to Local 47 of the Building Service Employees International Union would touch off a terrible two-year war, not only in the corridors of St. Luke's, but throughout all of Cleveland. The year was 1966. Nonprofit hospitals were still eight years away from being written into federal collective bargaining law, so there was no way to force hospital management to recognize a union it didn't want. Jim was an optimist by nature, but he also was a realist. From his father he had learned what it could mean to fight for unionization. He knew the hospital bosses would not be polite in their counterattack, and he knew workers might be forced to strike. And he knew that in a strike, many workers would suffer; some would lose their homes, families would be torn apart, people would go hungry, workers on both sides of the line might grow violent. So at that first meeting with Joe Murphy, then president of Local 47, and with other union officers at the Lancer Steak House, what Jim wanted most of all were assurances that the union would protect and support his people for the duration of the struggle. "I've got five hundred people out there," he told the union men. "You'd better be serious."

Satisfied that the international would stand by his workers, Jim accepted a thousand union authorization cards and went about the business of organizing. Through clandestine chats in the locker room, he rounded up a committee. He started working overtime so he could talk to people on different shifts and from different departments. "We had to move fast and quiet," he said. "I was in a hurry."

Within five months the union had managed to sign up almost all of the hospital's service employees. In the meantime Joe Murphy was working the political angle, meeting with hospital management and the Methodist clergy in an effort to convince them it would be best to recognize the union. But they wouldn't budge. The talks dragged on and on for more than a year, and still nothing. Then came the strike. One Tuesday afternoon at exactly one-thirty, five hundred hospital workers dropped what they were doing and marched down to the lobby. It was war.

Twenty-four hours a day seven days a week, picketers announced to the world that they wanted a union and vowed not to go back to work until the hospital agreed to negotiate. Outsiders joined in, uninvited, the Communist party and the Black Nationals, opportunists who saw the strike as a medium for their own political agenda. Fights broke out, a couple of homemade bombs went off. A court order was handed down, limiting strikers to three picketers per entrance. The community was outraged, terrified. The youngest and the oldest workers crossed the lines and went to work—the youngsters because they didn't understand, the older people out of fear. Still, the majority stuck to the strike: janitors, orderlies, aides, and food service workers all scraping by on their $25-a-week strike pay and charity from local churches and labor groups. Joe Murphy went to the Catholics, he went to the Methodists, and he went to Mayor Carl B. Stokes, the first black mayor of a major U.S. city, pleading for help. At last, in 1968, a year after the strike had begun, the Cleveland City Council passed a law requiring nonprofit hospitals in the city to hold a representation election if a majority of workers signed union authorization cards.

Victory.

A couple of months later Jim Horton was ordained an organizer for Local 47 and thrown right back into the trenches, this time in charge of nursing homes. Jim must have caught his adversary off guard, for he organized a dozen Cleveland-area homes in the first year. His pace slowed after that, but by the time he was named director of organizing in 1976, Jim Horton had brought workers from twenty nursing homes and twelve hospitals into the Local 47 fold. In the summer of 1980 he got a call from someone at the Copeland Oaks retirement home.

The sixty-mile drive out to Sebring lifted me into another world. With greater Cleveland far behind me, I meandered along narrow rustic roads that I had never even known about as a boy. For thirty miles along softly curved roadways my eyes feasted on the colors and patterns of the countryside: pastures and rolling hills, aging oaks and red-leafed maples, rickety fences and lazy cows, whitewashed farmhouses. My car—an old Chrysler my dad had bought for me—seemed to float. Silence enveloped the land, a silence at once earthy and divine, so filled with peace that the jabbering of my radio talk show seemed sacrilegious. I clicked off the radio and, for the first time in as long as I could remember, savored the feeling of solitude. For one glorious hour my mind had only the low rumble of the engine to distract it from its serenity. I chuckled to myself; it seemed proper that a retirement community would be built out on this road, along the pathway to Paradise.

My reverie was shattered by my arrival in Sebring. One look around and suddenly I wasn't feeling at all joyful. "Where the hell am I?" I said to myself. "And what am I doing there?"

Once the hub of Ohio's pottery industry, Sebring was now a patchwork of abandoned brick factories and boarded-up storefronts. The town proper was a two-block ghost town. I saw a dilapidated shop marked "Cafe" that appeared to have a couple of customers, and I noticed a well-stocked hardware store. But otherwise there were no signs of life. I cruised down the main street, peering up side roads. God, did anyone actually live there? I couldn't imagine. I checked my directions again, hoping that I had somehow missed Sebring and wound up in the wrong town. No such luck. I had started this trip hopeful that the Copeland Oaks job would buy me a new start in life. Now I was beginning to doubt that the place would be able to afford my $750 per diem. I checked the directions another time. I still had a couple of blocks before reaching the address; I'd just have to wait and see.

Then, out of nowhere, it appeared. Two stone pillars rose up from atop a low hill and stood guard over the entrance of an elegant estate. A cast-iron arch announced Copeland Oaks, a Cope Methodist Home. Beyond the columns, a long driveway stretched through the middle of a great green lawn, leading to a stately, colonial-style brick hall, its porch guarded by six whitewashed wooden columns. The large central building was surrounded by charming ranch-style homes, built of light orange brick, which were woven together with a maze of trim lawns and immaculate walkways. Beyond the buildings a blue lake shimmered in the amber autumn sun. The parking lot was discreetly tucked away to the side, so as not to intrude upon a visitor's view. A smile flitted across my lips. This was going to be okay.

The doors of the central building opened onto a magnificent foyer. The plush carpet muffled the buzz of a motorized wheelchair that carried a white-haired woman past formal sitting areas to the elevator. Two young women in crisp white knee-length dresses and thick-soled white shoes padded silently across the lobby, whispering serious secrets. They stepped into the elevator with the elderly woman and greeted her with cheery hellos. The door closed on the harmonic blend of the three voices.

I told the receptionist, who also smiled, that I had come to see Claude Roe. When I first contacted Claude he had given me the pat brush-off: "We already have a labor attorney." My months away from the action hadn't rusted me a bit, and I had responded enthusiastically:

"That's good to hear. I'm not a lawyer myself, and I wouldn't work without one. You need labor counsel."

That had bought me another minute. Then my supervisors-as-great-communicators pitch had rolled off my tongue as if I never had another thing on my mind, as if I had never been a desperate husband, an alcoholic, a criminal. I was sailing. Roe had seemed reassured by my confidence.

"You've tweaked my interest," he admitted. "Why don't you give my attorney a call."

I did, and I landed a meeting with Roe and attorney Lou Davies for the next day at Davies's office in Youngstown. The meeting was friendly; Roe and Davies seemed to like my approach. Still, Davies couldn't quite understand what I would be doing that he couldn't do just as well himself. So I applied a tactic that few salesmen—particularly union busters, who tend to be stingy and suspicious—are willing to use: I handed out free advice.

"Look," I said, "whether you hire me or not, there are certain things you should do to make sure you keep the advantage." Then I told them about the Excelsior list strategy, about not giving the complete names and addresses of employees on the list that they are required to prepare for the NLRB and the union. "Make it as hard as possible for the union to get to the people," I said.

They liked that. I was sent out of the room so Roe and Davies could talk things over. When I was called back in, Davies told me it had been the Excelsior list detail that clinched the sale.

Claude—"Dr. Roe" to his staff—came gliding through the lobby to greet me. He presented a most intimidating figure. A round, bald head rode stiffly on square shoulders atop a stately frame. The face was chiseled into a permanent scowl, the nose held at a slight upward angle in an expression of mild distaste for everything below. The body moved stiffly, frugally, as if every gesture had a sacred purpose. A Presbyterian minister and doctor of divinity who for career considerations was in the process of converting to the Methodist faith, Claude shunned his minister's costume, preferring the gray business suit of a banker. Affixed to his lapel was a small gold pin bearing the acronym MENSA. The brooch bore witness to Dr. Roe's membership in that international organization of the intellectually gifted and served as a constant reminder to all of his native superiority. Although I came to think of him as a sincere, if opaque, man, to Copeland Oaks workers Dr. Roe was considered stern and aloof. When the executive director greeted me with a pleasant look on his face and a crisp handshake, it was a rare show of enthusiasm that at the time I couldn't fully appreciate.

It was no secret that a decade earlier Copeland Oaks had stood on the brink of financial ruin. And it was no secret that Claude Roe had been the one to salvage it. When Claude was hired away from a string of Presbyterian nursing homes in New Jersey in 1972, Copeland was $11 million in the hole. The home reserved a large portion of its rooms for needy residents, who paid a fraction of the $500-$600 monthly fee out of their Social Security or Medicare income, with Copeland subsidizing the rest. Over the years those subsidies had become more and more of a burden to the facility. As a nonprofit home, Copeland did not have a steady source of income; it depended on donations and bequeathals from good-hearted citizens and grants from churches and foundations. Without constant rainmaking, the well had run dry. It took Claude six years to abolish Copeland's deficit, but by 1980—through a combination of higher fees, fewer subsidies, and endless, endless fund-raising—the home was enjoying a healthy annual surplus, known in commercial business as a profit.

Claude was clearly proud of Copeland's amenities—saw them as a personal tribute to him—so before we got down to business he took me on a tour of the kingdom. The elegance of the home continued to amaze me; I had worked at hospitals and nursing homes before, but this was different. The central building I had entered housed the Copeland corporate offices and a hundred residential apartments, but in decor and character it was more like a swank hotel. In addition to plush apartments and a regal sitting room, the main building boasted a lovely chapel, a dining room that was more elegant than most fine restaurants, and a recreation area that was a health club with billiard tables. A separate physical therapy room with specialized equipment and whirlpool bath was also available to the esteemed residents of Copeland.

Attached to the rear of the main building was the lumber-and-cement shell of a skilled-care facility that was then under construction. The new section, called Crandall Medical Center, was designed both as a hospital for current Copeland residents and as a home for other elderly people too feeble or ill for Copeland. Crandall was expected to be operating within a year, with Claude Roe as executive director.

Outside, strolling among the private homes—which Copeland called "villas"—I felt that I was a guest at an exclusive country club. I didn't mind revealing to him that I was impressed. "If I retire and have to go to a nursing home, this is where I want to be," I exclaimed. Claude knew the comforts of Copeland well. He and his wife lived in one of the more exclusive villas—for free.

Satisfied that I was sufficiently appreciative of Copeland's charm, Claude called a meeting with Davies. The executive director was clearly nervous. During the previous months, as Claude was all over northeastern Ohio meeting with church foundations, wealthy Christians, and other potential benefactors of his esteemed retirement home, Horton and his team of organizers had quietly spread the promise of a union to the weary Copeland employees. By fall Horton had assembled an inside organizing committee of thirty women and two men, which crusaded swiftly and silently for the support of the other workers. By the time Claude heard the rumblings, the union had signed up 60 percent of Copeland's hourly employees, about 170 nurses, nurse's aides, housekeepers, janitors, cooks, and waitresses. Signed authorization cards at the ready, Jim Horton had put in a call to Dr. Roe.

It was a phone call Claude will never forget, for it was the opening salvo of a nasty nineteen-month war. Horton was brief and courteous. He told Dr. Roe that Copeland employees had expressed an interest in union representation and asked for a meeting with the director so he could prove that a majority of employees had signed authorization cards. If Dr. Roe would agree voluntarily to recognize the union, both sides could save themselves the trouble and expense of an NLRB election, and they could get right to work on negotiating a contract.

Well, Dr. Roe had no intention of meeting, and he certainly wasn't negotiating any contract. Why should he? The union was after him, not the other way around. He didn't need a union, and he didn't want one; it was just going to cost him money and get in his way. He couldn't see how he had anything to gain by sitting down with union people. No, Mr. Horton, said Claude. There will be no meeting. We have nothing to discuss. If the union wants Copeland Oaks, it is going to have to come and get it.

Claude's pronouncement that the union was going to have to fight for Copeland was a perversion of the truth so sublime that most people would not catch it; possibly even Claude himself was unaware of the deception. The truth is, unions do not fight to "get" workers. They fight on behalf of workers. At Copeland the truth was employees were asking the union to represent them, not the other way around. The truth was Copeland workers had called Local 47, not the other way around. The truth was Copeland workers were unhappy with their treatment and wanted changes. The truth was Horton and the other organizers were trying to help Copeland employees get what the employees wanted, which was an organization that would look out for their interests. The truth was in vowing to fight the union, Claude was vowing to fight his own employees, to do battle with laundrywomen and maids and cooks.

Funny thing was, Claude thought himself a kind man. Really.

He announced proudly that Copeland paid as well as the other retirement homes in the area—that is to say, a few pennies above the minimum wage—despite a history of horrific financial trouble. He boasted that the employees were like family to one another, as if that were somehow his doing. There were fewer than three hundred workers at Copeland, most of them simple, modest women from Sebring and the surrounding towns and villages. They knew each other's children, they shared each other's secrets, they attended each other's Christmas parties. Claude himself claimed to know all his employees by name, although I never saw him greet any of his subordinates, by name or otherwise. Amazingly, he imagined that he was loved and respected and believed that the employees thought of him in fatherly terms. He was appalled at the suggestion that he had not done enough for them. If that union really thought it could turn his girls against him, well, it was welcome to try.

Claude, Lou Davies, and I locked ourselves in Claude's office for our first strategy session. Before we began drawing battle plans, I turned to Claude and offered my congratulations for his having sidestepped the first of what I called union "traps": the proposed meeting. Claude's refusal to meet with Horton had been impetuous, I knew, driven by ego, not wiles. He was raw, a union hater to be sure, but not an educated one. Now his schooling was about to begin. First lesson: The union must always be thought of—and publicized—as devious. Every move must be interpreted as sneaky, every motive treated as suspect. I told Claude that Horton's meeting invitation had been a ploy to trick him into recognizing the union. Unions will do that, you know, I said. They'll slither up to you with some pretense or other, then they'll stick a pile of authorization cards under your nose, and before you know it you've bought yourself a union. Thank goodness you had the instincts to run, Claude, for had you not, you might be sitting across the table from the SEIU right now instead of me.

Claude gasped. How could that be? he asked.

Here's how, I said: if, being a good-hearted and fair man, you had sat down with union organizers on Copeland Oaks premises, you would have taken one step toward recognizing the union. If, being a reasonable man, you had taken them up on their offer to look at the authorization cards, you could have automatically waived your so-called "good-faith doubt" that the union had the support of a majority of the workers, and the NLRB could have ordered you to negotiate. Imagine! The union would have snuck right in under your nose.

Claude let out a stream of air he seemed to have forgotten about. Good for you for not falling for that one, I told him. But watch out, this was just the first trick. There will be hundreds of land mines buried along the way. Unions are desperate for members, and they'll resort to all kinds of chicanery to fill their rosters. That is why you must not say or do anything in this campaign without checking with Mr. Davies and me.

Claude looked grateful. He was all mine.

What I told Claude, and later all the Copeland supervisors, and all supervisors in every anti-union campaign, was another perverted truth. I started with the facts of the law, then put a spin on them to make the whole process seem quite unholy. Yes, labor law does allow unions and employers to agree on union recognition without going to an NLRB election. In fact, before the NLRB will even accept a union's petition for an election, the union must already have asked management if it will recognize the union voluntarily. It has to ask. Louis Celaya asked Ed Daly. He had to. Later, Jim White would ask Mike Puskarich at Cravat Coal. He would have to. Horton asked Roe. He had to.

Companies wishing to save some money and avoid the antagonism generated during a representation election campaign can answer "Yes" and agree to recognize the union by checking the authorization cards in the presence of a neutral witness, thereby acknowledging that the union represents the majority of workers. It's very simple, and it's very cheap. And it's almost never done. Why? Because bosses don't want to negotiate with their workers, that's why.

Now, suppose a card check, as the process is called, did not automatically constitute recognition of the union. What would happen? Well, management would jump at the chance to see the cards, wouldn't it? What anti-union boss wouldn't love to have a peek at union authorization cards and get the names of all those sonsofbitches who signed them? After its little reconnaissance mission, management could tell the union, Forget it, no deal, and go back to the company and kick butt. How could the union protect the employees who had signed cards? It couldn't. And how could the union ever win an election? It couldn't. So the law seeks to ensure that bosses will not play dangerous card games by prescribing that, under certain conditions, a supervisor's looking at authorization cards may constitute de facto recognition. Naturally my clients never heard the truthful version of the law, nor did they care to. When you're at war you do well not to identify with your enemy.

With my little band huddled around me in Claude's office, I scanned the SEIU petition for clues to my opening strike. As expected, I found an opening in the union's definition of the bargaining unit.

Local 47 sought to represent more than 250 Copeland workers, all the facility's housekeepers, laundrywomen, maintenance men, cooks, waitresses, dishwashers, nurse's aides, beauticians, and vocational nurses. That left me only about a dozen executives, department heads, RNs, and miscellaneous office people to carry out my counter-campaign. At a glance I knew that wouldn't do. There was no way I could count on a handful of supervisors—and I had to assume some of them would side with their workers—to conquer twenty times that number of employees. Not with a strategy that turned on direct, one-on-one confrontations with the workers. The more frequent and more intense those confrontations, the greater the chances that my troops would succeed in breaking the workers' resolve. As a general rule, I juggled bargaining units so that no supervisor would have to handle more than fifteen subordinates. I would do the same at Copeland; the only question was where to strike.

Nurse's aides made up the largest employee group; the SEIU petition put the number at ninety. Claude suspected that the aides also were the most solidly pro-union, and it turned out he was right. Yet Copeland's nursing management consisted of one director of nursing and just three RNs. I knew four people would never be able to grind down that many union supporters no matter how earnestly they carried out my campaign. They were going to need help. I zeroed in on the thirty vocational nurses, called LPNs (for licensed practical nurses). I had worked hospital campaigns before, so I knew the general hierarchy of the nursing world. It was a running joke inside hospitals that RN stands for "real nurses" and LPN means "let's pretend nurses." But in terms of what most people think of as nursing, down-and-dirty patient care, the real work is done by the LPNs. Copeland's LPNs were responsible for the day-to-day care of the residents; the RNs administered the drugs, and the LPNs did just about everything else. They dressed the wounds, exercised the limbs, drew the blood, took the temperature, fed the mouths, and listened and listened and listened. And they wanted a union. Several LPNs had been involved in the organizing from the beginning, and a few still were part of Horton's organizing committee, which met weekly at a coffee shop in the town of Alliance, thirty miles east of Sebring.

There was little to suggest that LPNs should be considered part of management, but I needed them and I deemed that they would be. Because there were only three RNs at Copeland, I knew the nurse's aides answered directly to the LPNs. The LPNs were the ones who told the aides when a patient needed to be taken to the toilet or bathed or fed or when bed pans had to be emptied or messes needed to be cleaned up. That was a start. I also learned that at Copeland some LPNs were designated as "charge" nurses, meaning they were in charge of the swing shift or the graveyard shift on a particular day. That was even better. In truth, just because a worker sometimes directs the activities of another does not mean she should automatically be excluded from a union. But the ambiguous language of labor law regarding the definition of a supervisor leaves plenty of room for games. I was a good player, and I knew I had a chance at capturing the LPNs. According to the National Labor Relations Act, a supervisor is someone who can hire, fire, or transfer employees or—and here are the magic words—"who can effectively recommend" any of those things. All we would have to do is argue that the LPNs could make recommendations about the duties and assignments of their aides.

I told Davies we needed to get the LPNs designated as supervisors if we were to have a chance to defuse the organizing drive. Davies was doubtful. It would be difficult, he said, shaking his head; there was no legal precedent. Nevertheless, he conceded that I had provided him with a logical argument and said he'd be glad to give it a whirl. I smiled. It was going to be a pleasure working with Davies, I decided. He was serious and professional, a fine attorney from a traditional Youngstown law firm. But he was obviously willing to try new things.

As Davies prepared to go to hearing on the unit issue, I launched my campaign. I set a kick-off for the next day, in the home's Williamsburg Lounge, a cozy sitting room adjacent to the chapel. Naturally I wouldn't be letting the LPNs in on the meeting while they were still part of the union movement, so my kick-off would be an unusually intimate affair, including only the twelve managers I knew I had. If the board found in my favor, terrific; I'd do another kick-off for the LPNs. If not, well, I was in trouble, and I'd better get started. When Davies filed his objection to the voting unit, he simultaneously filed a challenge to the jurisdiction of the NLRB at Copeland. It was a bread-and-butter delay tactic to argue that the labor board had no business overseeing union elections at a company for some obscure legal reason. But the stratagem was no less effective for its ordinariness. As long as the board went on debating and deliberating on that issue, the union would not get the Excelsior list, making it hard for them to contact all the potential voters, and no election date would be set. All the while, we would have the run of the place.

The board's ruling came fast, in less than a week. Although the union had fought the reclassifying of LPNs as supervisors, the NLRB saw it our way. I got them. The LPNs were mine. I relished the victory even though I knew it was a mixed one. Throughout all my years running anti-union drives, I never found a group of supervisors more resentful of my campaigns than nurses. As a class I have found nurses difficult and ornery; considering what I was all about, that is very much to their credit. Nurses, no matter how low paid, consider themselves professionals. The way they see it, their job is to care for the patients, period. They do not willingly accept assignments that interfere with that sacred mission. Typically, nurses resist even those administrative and managerial tasks that are part of the usual health care routine. When burdened with a duty as imposing and obnoxious as an anti-union drive, they can be positively defiant. And when it so happens that the nursing staff is overwhelmingly in favor of organizing— as it was at Copeland— they can make a real mess of things. And I have to be particularly nasty. I knew my brigade of newly drafted LPNs would be troublesome. Nonetheless, their conscription into the ranks of management gave me the numbers I needed and, if nothing else, automatically robbed the union of a few dozen votes.

As soon as Lou Davies told me the nurses were in, I skipped over to Claude's office. The LPN issue was a delicate one, and I had to make sure that word got out in just the right way. We didn't want the nurses thinking for a moment that management had pulled a fast one. Oh, gosh, no. It was time for a little preventive PR.

My yellow legal pad in hand, I sat down with Claude and composed a letter in longhand. It was addressed to the licensed practical nurses at Copeland Oaks retirement home and phrased very neatly. The language was dry, a la Claude Roe, but the tone was a bit warmer. The letter informed the nurses that they had been determined by the federal government to be supervisors. The words implied innocence on the part of Copeland management, which was portrayed as astonished by the revelation that the federal government, not the administration, got to decide who was a supervisor and who was not. The letter then waxed humble, recognizing that the management had no choice but to obey the law. In that spirit, the letter went on to explain that the role of supervisor brought with it certain obligations, not the least of which was loyalty to the company. Therefore Copeland would dutifully incorporate the newly knighted LPNs into management's pro-company campaign. I passed the pad to Claude, who gave the letter a quick reading, then looked at me with a quizzical smirk.

"I want the nurses to hear that we're not manipulating them," I told him, pronouncing the word manipulating with special care. He nodded.

I took my composition to Claude's secretary, Betty Miller, and asked her to type it up on a Copeland-Crandall letterhead. Then Claude signed his name importantly at the bottom.

The next afternoon, the letter having been distributed and, no doubt, much commented on, the nurses filed silently into the Williamsburg Lounge. They held their eyes steady, their faces stiff and expressionless. Dressed in crisp white pantsuits and dresses, they ranged in age from their late teens to their late fifties. I sensed their strength at once. They didn't seem hostile, really. No, they were tougher than that. Hostile is easy. I can take hostile and twist it back on itself with a few quick moves. But I could see that first day that the Copeland nurses were a little more wily, a little more in control, than most groups of unwilling managers. Their opaque expressions and occasional smirks told me they were impervious to my exhortations and only mildly entertained by my cleverness. As I paced the room quizzing the crowd, I silently evaluated my students' anti-union IQ and made a mental list of potential troublemakers. The list was long.

In the beginning, some of the most vocal support for the union came from the LPNs. They contributed to the strategy meetings, they helped pass out authorization cards. Their familiarity with the workings and personalities of Copeland and their understanding of the nursing home business had given SEIU organizers the kind of detailed intelligence that is invaluable to a union effort and very difficult to obtain. The nurses were determined to get that union. They felt they were neither paid nor respected as skilled professionals. Tasks and shifts were assigned, perquisites and punishments meted out, at the whim of the trio of RNs who ran Copeland's medical department, the director of nursing, and her assistants. Accordingly, the quality of each nurse's work life depended on the personal rapport she maintained with three distant and, some said, hostile administrators. A chosen few had it made. The rest suffered.

But the moment they were drafted into management, the LPNs had to give up the union meetings. At the kick-off I warned them that they could be fired for attending. Not Copeland's rule, mind you, but the federal government's rule on surveillance. I told the LPNs they didn't dare go anywhere near the organizing meetings, no matter how close their friendships with the union "pushers." Friendship could be very dangerous at times like these, I said. In war alliances had to be redefined. The nurses were management now, and they had to be careful not to let their emotional ties lead them into a union trap that could harm the company. I taught the nurses the facts of the law: that management presence at union meetings destroys the "laboratory conditions" in which the NLRB insists that union-organizing campaigns take place and thus risks an unfair labor practice charge against the company. If any of them were to let that happen, I said, she would be held responsible. She would be fired.

Naturally my main interest in keeping the nurses away from union meetings was to deny organizers their support and their information. But this time I had labor law on my side. What I told them was essentially true. What I didn't tell them was that I had nothing at all against spying. When I needed spies I would send in my anti-union rank and file, my circle pluses, my grunts. Perfectly legitimate.

I knew my hold on this new group of hostages was tenuous, no matter how powerful my performance, so I decided to set them to work right away. I had started my letter campaign without the nurses, but now that they were mine I wanted them involved every second. Before releasing the LPNs, I gave them their first assignment. I passed out a letter written in question-and-answer format, an old trick I used to create the illusion that an actual dialogue was taking place. The opening read:

Dear Staff Member: Several of you have been asking some very important questions concerning the current union situation. Here are the factual answers to your questions:

Following were three questions and Claude's—that is, my— lengthy and emphatic answers. Of course, no employee had asked a thing. I had made those questions up, a fact of which Claude might or might not have been aware. As controller of information, I regulated not only what the employees were told, but when they were told it, by whom, and in what form. I certainly wasn't going to wait for a bunch of cooks and maids to ask the right question at the right time in the right way. In that very early letter, I began my ground war against the integrity of collective bargaining, the heart of union representation. With cunningly worded answers to contrived questions, I presented collective bargaining as a protracted, risky, and possibly futile process and warned employees that "unions have been known to trade away whatever it takes" to win costly little plums for themselves.

That first Q&A letter walked a tightrope over the realm of the unlawful. For example, had I written, "Bargaining starts from scratch," my letter would have been illegal and the union could have filed an unfair labor practice complaint. That's because those exact words have been tested in the courts and determined to be against the laws that govern representation elections. So, big deal, I picked other words. But I said the same thing. I wrote, "Nothing is automatic in a union contract. Everything is subject to bargaining (horse trading). ..."

It is also illegal for a company to refuse to bargain with a union that has been duly elected by the workers. So I didn't say Copeland would refuse. I just let the readers know that the company would make it very hard on the union to win anything. I wrote: "We would not be obliged to agree to anything or to make any concessions. ..."

Before taking the letter to Claude for his signature, I cleared it with Lou Davies. I didn't mind breaking the law, but things would go so much more smoothly if we could just slither in and out of the loopholes. Davies said it was fine. The letter closed with the admonition, "Remember: A bird in the hand is worth two in the bush." Trite, but crystal clear.

Later on in the campaign I had Claude set up a question box by the time clock. I designed the box—a shoebox-size container covered with white paper and decorated with big red question marks, with a slot on the top through which discreet questioners could deposit their queries on folded scraps of paper. Claude then invited all employees to use the box to ask questions about the union drive—anonymity guaranteed. It was a revival of an old Sheridan trick. Perhaps the box actually would attract a question or two that would point to some frailty in the organizing effort or show us what the workers feared. Handy, but that wasn't the point. The question box really served as a cover for my tightly orchestrated information campaign; I made up most of the questions myself. In my earlier years I had occasionally been challenged upon claiming that workers had been asking a certain question. A feisty supervisor would stand up in a meeting and complain, "Wait a minute. I never heard anybody out there ask that. Just who do you say is asking that question?" or something similar. I would always have an out in claiming respect for the purported inquisitor's privacy and refuse to identify him, but the confrontation itself was undesirable. It planted the possibility in the minds of otherwise docile supervisors that upper management might, in fact, be scamming them. With the question box in place, no one would know who was asking what, and I could float "questions from the employees" as I saw fit. Any doubt about the legitimacy of the inquiries would be limited to some private mutterings.

I was living in two worlds during those early days of Copeland. By day I played the heavy. I held the fate of nearly three hundred workers in my hands, and I gave the orders. I handed out praise and punishment as I saw fit, showing mercy one moment, ruthlessness the next. But when night fell I was a little boy again. Back at my parents' house I sat in the family room, watched TV, smoked, played with my nail clipper, drank Scotch, scratched cryptic calculations on my legal pad, and telephoned Alice. After begging and pleading with her every night for nearly a month, I could tell she was beginning to relent. She started talking about wanting to get away from the cult, away from Scott. Yes, she said, maybe we should try to be a family again. God knew the boys could use having you around. But she was afraid. What if he didn't let her go? He had said he intended to marry her. What if he came after her? He could be pretty scary. Besides, she said, she didn't have the money to move all our stuff.

Then I got a brilliant idea. Alice was glad I was working, but that wasn't enough to get her to move away from her mom and dad. But if she had a job as well, she might do it. "Alice," I said, "I could really use some help on this campaign. There are too many supervisors for me to handle alone. Most of them are women, and I get the feeling some of them would be more comfortable talking to a woman. You'd be perfect. You're sweet, you're compassionate, I'm sure they'd open up to you in a way they just won't to me. I can tell some of them are holding back."

Alice was intrigued. She was a torn woman, restless from being home all the time yet committed to her fantasy of being the storybook wife and mother, which required her to be home all the time. She also was held back by her poor self-image. She couldn't imagine who would want to hire her, and she never tried to find out. But one thing I knew she was good at, and that was nurturing. Alice was a caring mother, a talented and energetic homemaker, a gifted gardener, a giving friend. She was even an enthusiastic wife when times were good. I figured I could parlay all that native empathy into a stint at Copeland.

"To hell with Scott," I said. "He wants to marry you? Well, I already did that, and I'm the one who doesn't want to let you go. Come back to me. We can work together like we did in the old days. I love you. I love you, Alice. I need you."

At long last, Alice gave in. All right, she said. Get the money for the move and I will fly out with the boys. We'll be there before Christmas.

I had sold Copeland Oaks at my going rate of $750 a day, and the campaign promised to last a few months at least; I knew I had money coming. But because my sales pitch had been somewhat a show of self-assurance, I hadn't wanted to ask Claude for a retainer. So I was still as broke as the day I had left California.

During the early weeks of the campaign, Claude and I had become quite good friends. Wherever I was, I liked to develop a personal relationship with the top man; it helped me retain control by averting resentment. But with Claude, the relationship grew more rapidly than usual. I often spent the afternoons in long conversations with him that inevitably grew quite intimate. I felt comfortable revealing my sins to him, undoubtedly seduced by his station as a man of the cloth. When I stepped into his office and closed the door, it was as if I had entered the confessional. I barely knew Claude when I began telling him about Alice's affairs and my drinking and our constant warring. He listened and counseled and consoled and seemed earnest about his desire to help me straighten out my life. He had been married to his wife, Gladys, for four decades, and still seemed very much taken with her. He said often that he wished I would someday know the happiness that came from a long, enduring marriage. When I appeared in his office one December morning and asked if he could pay me a ten-day advance so that I could move my family out to Cleveland, Claude didn't hesitate.

The executive director called in his comptroller and ordered him to draw me up a check for $7,500. Immediately.

I didn't have a bank account and, after my bank shenanigans in California, had little hope of getting one. I was still puzzling over how to cash Claude's check when a moving van pulled up in front of my parents' house.

Alice and the boys had made it to my parents' house a week before Christmas.

Within a couple of weeks I had identified the few supervisors who were willing to work extra hard for me—or, as they put it, "for the home." Through that handful of good soldiers I set to work establishing a network of rank-and-file employees who would serve as spies, informants, and saboteurs. Those so-called loyal employees would be called upon to lobby against the union, report on union meetings, hand over union literature to their bosses, tattle on their co-workers, help spread rumors, and make general pests of themselves within the organizing drive. I rarely knew who my company plants were, and I didn't at Copeland. It was cleaner that way. Nobody could connect me to the activities, I steered clear of the reporting requirements of Landrum-Griffin, and the workers' "pro-company" counter-campaign was believed to be a grass-roots movement.

My intelligence network informed me early on that, although Jim Horton was the man in charge of the Copeland drive, and probably had a lot to do with the campaign's methodology, he was not the most visible organizer. Horton and four other union officers cooperated in the Copeland effort that drive being one of the biggest ever for Local 47. The name known to most of the workers was Phil Ganni.

Ganni, a gruff old man with a round belly, was an interesting anomaly. He was not an organizer, not on staff at Local 47, not even a member, not a Copeland employee. He was, quite simply, a good friend. Ganni was a former Sebring autoworker on permanent disability, and he was a devoted union man. Many of the women who worked at Copeland happened to live in his Alliance neighborhood, and he talked with them often about their jobs and their troubles. When the women started asking him how to go about getting a union, Ganni said he'd be glad to help. It was Ganni who placed that first call to Local 47 in the summer of 1980. It was Ganni who first met with Horton at an Alliance coffee shop to talk strategy. It was Ganni who first started assembling an organizing committee through his neighborhood friends. It was Ganni, more than anyone else in the early days, who went knocking on doors and setting up meetings and making phone calls to his friends. After the union petition was filed in late November, Ganni stayed on, working as a link between the union organizers in Cleveland and his friends in Sebring and Alliance. To the women at Copeland, Ganni was quarterback, coach, and cheerleader all rolled into one. For many weeks he worked the organizing effort as a volunteer, putting in full days and long nights out of sheer conviction. Eventually Local 47 paid him a stipend for his trouble.

From the reading I was getting through my supervisors, Local 47 was running a straight campaign, nothing dirty, no wild promises, no rabble-rousing. I was always grateful when a few union people did something really tacky or really stupid, like start a fight or slash somebody's tires; it made things so easy. All I had to do was say, "Just look. Are those the kind of people you want representing you?" But it wasn't going to be like that at Copeland. I was going to have to commit Local 47's sins myself.

One target was Ganni. I never used his name, didn't throw too big a spotlight on him. I had been told that the Copeland workers generally liked and respected Ganni, those who knew him, so I knew an all-out attack on him would be unwise. But I also knew that some of the women considered Ganni somewhat of a blow-hard; they had been heard wondering aloud, "Who does he think he is?" That gave me an opening, not to topple him—he wasn't that important—just to nurture the germ of doubt about him that already existed.

I started spreading the word through supervisors that Local 47 apparently couldn't handle the Copeland organizing drive itself. It had come to my attention, I told them, that the union was paying someone to go after the "pro-company" employees. What kind of a dirty trick was that? I asked. Just like a union. When things start getting rough, send in a goon. I began referring to Ganni as the union's "paid bounty hunter from Alliance" and eventually included that reference in a letter. This bounty hunter, I wrote, was working in collusion with "inside union pushers" and "high-paid professional unionists from up in Cleveland," all of whom *have lied to you in their efforts to fill their pockets with your money.*" In that way I painted a picture of the cold, corrupt, big-business union that so many of my victims had heard about ad nauseam growing up in the small towns of the Midwest. Of course, those union types were lying, I implied. Whenever I mentioned the union people, I was sure to note that they came from far away in the big city. Big cities mean bad guys, crime, sleaze, big money, Mafia.

For the record, as director of organizing Jim Horton was paid about $600 a week in 1980; his fellow organizers earned slightly less. An okay salary, but for a man of fifty-two hardly big money. I never found out what Ganni was paid.

Ganni's closest contact within the union was not Horton, but another black man, Art Worthy. Soft spoken and earnest, Worthy won Ganni's trust immediately, and he became the union face to Copeland workers. When Ganni sent letters to the local, they were addressed to Art Worthy. When he set up meetings, he made sure Worthy would be there. When he called, he wanted to talk to Art. Worthy had gotten into organizing during the 1960s, after working as a construction laborer for many years. His first organizing jobs were with the Construction Laborers Union, but he switched to hospitals in 1971 in order to help Local 47 bring a union to service workers at Huron Road Hospital in East Cleveland, where many of his relatives toiled. Worthy stayed with Local 47 after winning Huron, and he even worked for a time as business representative to St. Luke's, Horton's old stamping grounds. Worthy and Horton got on well, and although there were three other field organizers assigned to Copeland, the campaign was essentially theirs.

Every week Horton or Worthy sat down to discuss strategy with the thirty-odd inside organizers from Copeland. The duo also ran union rallies and informational meetings at hotel meeting rooms and restaurants in Sebring, Alliance, and the surrounding towns, and they put out union circulars. The organizers from Local 47 kept in touch with Copeland workers the best it could, with the dogged assistance of Ganni, and tried their damnedest to defuse the hostility and defend their union against the charges being launched daily under the name of Claude L. Roe.

From their years on the front lines, Horton and Worthy had developed a very definite organizing style and a strong sense of strategy. The first rule was Stick to your own game. Horton was adamant about it. You don't let the company and you certainly don't let a hired union buster dictate the issues and determine the direction of your own organizing campaign. It's a good rule, a smart rule. But it's also a difficult one to follow, impossible if there's someone like Marty Levitt on the inside, immersing the workers hour by hour in the issues he wants to address. The union doesn't get to come inside. The union gets to talk to the workers only after they've heard eight hours' worth of the other side, sometimes accompanied by threats, sometimes by tears.

"[Copeland] was the toughest campaign I've ever done—the most painful," Horton said years later. The reason: Organizers seemed always to be following my lead, always responding to charges, always defending the union. At Copeland Horton never had a chance to run the organizing campaign the way he knew it should be run. Not that it was the first time he had come across a professional union buster. He had dealt with union busters many times before, had lost a lot, but also had beaten them often enough to figure he knew their game. Horton and his fellow organizers had gone to workshops on union busters, seen films, planned counter-strategies. He knew enough to warn union supporters at the early Copeland meetings, "Watch out. Whoever's writing the letters for management is going to put half-truths in there, just enough so it's not a lie." The union buster Horton knew best was a fellow named Jack Hickey, an independent consultant based in Columbus who had followed Local 47 from campaign to campaign for years. Hickey's style was rougher than mine. He routinely called in security guards to intimidate workers, for example. Hickey was brusque, and, according to Horton, "turned people off along the way." But organizers had yet to experience the Sheridan cum Three M cum Levitt war of saturation bombing, and I caught them quite unprepared.

"[Marty] confused the workers. ... He got them doubting us, challenging us, using up our meeting rime," Horton said.

A union meeting might go two, three, four hours. More often than not, during the Copeland effort, Horton and Worthy were forced to spend that time straightening out the twisted disinformation sown by me.

"Marty put us on the defensive," said Horton. "Some of the rank-and-file workers knew his name. But most of them just knew him as 'that man,' the man they had heard about from their supervisors. They would always say, 'That man, he told us this. . . . ' He would always say something halfway. He might leave out something or make one little change that would make what he said wrong. Then we'd have to spend the whole meeting explaining it."

In the end, maybe the people's immediate questions would be answered, maybe. But there would be more to come, and more, and more, ad infinitum. Of equal importance to me, organizers would have had no time for planning, no time for campaign strategy, no time for talking about the issues that really concerned the workers. The union would have gone nowhere.

Copeland's cleaning crew was a tight-knit and hardworking group. Every morning at 7 A.M., as the day shift came on, the group of eighteen housekeepers and laundrywomen met in the ladies' locker room. There they received their assignments for the day and discussed any special preparations that had to be made. The meeting was routine, but to the women there was something very comforting about starting the day together like that. It was a time of laughter and gossip, and it gave the crew a jump-start at the top of a day of hard, dirty work. It was a cherished time. After the meeting the housekeeping crew split up in pairs and scrubbed and polished and vacuumed its way through every apartment and villa in the complex, in an energetic endeavor to defend Copeland's reputation as the cleanest retirement home in the area.

Presiding over the morning roll call like a stern but loving mother superior was Kathleen Taylor, director of housekeeping and laundry. Kathleen was an odd, rather anachronistic character. She covered her tidy matronly figure in prim frocks adorned with the lace cuffs and high button-up collars of the previous century. She always kept an embroidered cloth hankie tucked neatly under one cuff. From our first conversation Kathleen painted herself as the beloved auntie to all her employees, to whom she referred as her "girls." She took care of them, she said, mothered them. Kathleen treasured the morning roll call perhaps even more than her crew; she took personal pride in the quality of her "girls' " work— and personal interest in the details of their lives. She relished the gossip, the confessions, the conspiracies, the glimpse inside the homes of each of her subordinates. And she imagined that her "girls" loved her in return.

She was wrong. Although Kathleen had a couple of loyal friends among her crew, my conversations with her co-workers revealed that by and large, the girls scorned her. They considered her mothering overbearing and intrusive, her leadership autocratic and arbitrary, and her personal style ridiculous. They said she played favorites. They called her a busybody, a snob, and a witch.

There is an element of truth in almost everything the union buster says. One of the truths is that where an organizing drive is taking place, one will invariably find lousy supervision. Kathleen was a dedicated employee, a loyal soldier; but she was one crummy supervisor. She was bossy, she was manipulative, she was nosy, and she was unfair. The trouble was, she didn't know it. Cope-land's housekeeping crew was a feisty bunch, outspoken and unafraid and, from what I could tell, quite solidly behind the organizing drive. I wasn't going to have Kathleen fired; the girls didn't hate her enough for that to have been useful. But I knew I had to wake her up from her delusion if she was going to do me any good.

"Kathleen, do you know what your girls are saying about you?" I asked her during a one-on-one session a few weeks into the campaign. She couldn't imagine. I held her eyes with mine and said with a tone of pity: "You're a fool if you think your girls look up to you. They don't even like you. In fact, they laugh at you. They even make fun of the way you dress, did you know that? The lace and the high collars, and the hankie and all. They call you a snob. They say you think you're a fashion plate, and they mimic the way you talk. I hope you don't think those girls will be loyal to you. They won't. They're stabbing you in the back right now."

Kathleen was dumbfounded. How could it be? How could she not see it? She had always treated the girls the way she would want to be treated if their roles were reversed, hadn't she? She showed them respect, and they respected her in return. Didn't they? Kathleen's eyes filled. She pulled the hankie from her sleeve and dabbed the tears, sniffing to hold back a full-blown cry. She was all mine.

"Look, Kathleen," I offered. "You still have a chance to make amends to your girls. Talk to them. Find out what it is you've done to make them call in the union and tell them you're willing to change. Assure them that they can come to you with any complaint, and let them know you'll really listen. Apologize for any mistakes you've made, even if you don't know what they are." Then my voice turned hard. "At the same time, be sure they know this: It's a onetime offer. Warn them that once the union takes over it's out of your hands. From that moment on there will be no more flexibility, no more chances for change. Everything will be regimented, impersonal. Tell them that they won't be able to speak for themselves, and you won't be allowed to answer. Every little detail of their workday will be determined by some union man up in Cleveland."

That did it. Kathleen would do anything to fight off this personal attack. She would do anything to defeat the monster that would take her workers away from her. I was sure she would not stray; I was equally sure she would not be very effective. I would have to work around her.

After a month or so at Copeland I found myself having to work around quite a number of management people, not the least of whom was Claude L. Roe. As is true at most companies, the poor supervision on the floor of Copeland Oaks was more than a matter of a few bad hires. The trouble was endemic to the organization and would not be cleared up with a couple of training workshops. Rather, Copeland's erratic supervision was a symptom of a diseased organization; the disease spread downward, from a cancer afflicting the top.

One after the other, the supervisors hinted at it. "Dr. Roe, he's so . . . smart. People are afraid to talk to him." "The girls don't. . . feel very comfortable around him." "He doesn't seem to, well, care very much about us." But it was Claude's secretary, Betty Miller, who made me see just how much the employees dreaded her boss. Betty was likable and intelligent. She had the run of Copeland; she saw things; she heard things. What she heard most was that Dr. Roe was quite unanimously despised. The girls thought he was mean and sour. His presence was oppressive. Everyone was happiest when he was away. I tried, I tried my damnedest to lighten Claude up, get him at least to greet people when he was packed into an elevator with them. But to no avail. I couldn't even talk Claude into opening his anti-union letters with "Dear Fellow Employee." Too cozy, unprofessional. Claude did not consider himself a "fellow" to any of the workers. He was their boss, and they were his staff.

Because of his refusal to bow his head even slightly, I found it necessary to pop open my "Give us a chance" letter earlier in the Copeland campaign than I would have liked. Ever since World Airways, the tearful, apologetic plea had become a mainstay of the final days of my campaigns. The letter tended to be most effective at that time, when everybody was exhausted from the fight and therefore vulnerable to an apparent call for a truce. I decided not to take chances with Claude. I packaged the plea into his third letter, being careful not to give it too much emphasis lest it be recognized for the ploy that it was. Claude's "we are not perfect" passage followed the claim that he was not afraid of the union, along with a trio of lies that purported to explain why, in that case, Copeland management was fighting so hard to defeat it.

"WE ARE CONCERNED," I wrote.
"WE ARE CONCERNED that a self-serving group of outsiders does not trick you into putting your future on a bargaining table.
"WE ARE CONCERNED about seeing you give up your individual right to speak for yourself.
"WE ARE CONCERNED about losing the proud tradition of direct relationships and flexibility that has allowed Copeland Oaks to be so very special."

Then came a brief admission that Copeland management might, indeed, have made some mistakes and the declaration, "But we genuinely believe we deserve a chance.

It was total crap. Claude was not concerned, he was afraid and he was angry. Union representation did not threaten to deprive the employees of any of their so-called proud traditions, if there were any, but it did threaten to deprive Claude of his autocracy.

I never stopped trying to soften Claude's severe bearing. I began to see the old grump as an amusing puzzle; it was a personal challenge to make him laugh—hell, smile even. But I wasn't going to risk my campaign for a little fun. So while I scratched away at Claude's opaqueness, I enlisted a pair of his top aides to be the face of Copeland to the people.

My ace was Bill Hogg, the home's resident Methodist minister and the director of community relations. Bill was friendly and warm—naturally. Unlike Claude, who liked to hole himself up in his executive suite, Bill spent his days roaming the halls of Copeland Oaks, visiting residents, chatting with the workers, conducting chapel service. I heard often in my interviews that the girls wished Bill Hogg were the director instead of Dr. Roe. Bill—they called him Bill—joked with them, ate with them, was one of them, really. Except that Bill was also a good company man, and that meant he would fight their organizing drive.

I had Claude sign the letters to employees. But when it came to personal appeals, I sent Bill. Bill's whole shtick was bridge building—that's what community relations was all about. He brought people together to sup in peace. When Bill characterized the union as an invader that would tear friends apart, people listened. I knew they would listen even better if God could be insinuated into the fight. So I arranged for a pivotal staff meeting to be scheduled in the Copeland chapel. There, Bill delivered a most eloquent, most passionate anti-union homily from the pulpit.

Helping Bill out with any gender-related issues was Gerry Sposato, Claude's assistant director. Gerry was a dour, straitlaced lady in her early forties, drab, proper, and hardly fun loving. She did not really fit my job description for the new, reformed manager, but she was useful in her own way. Gerry knew a great deal about Copeland, about Claude, about her fellow supervisors, and about the workers. She was the first to tell me what the housekeepers thought of Kathleen; she also informed me that the nurses felt oppressed by their boss, Anna Moracco, and knew the complaints of the kitchen staff. Gerry knew how things worked, who influenced whom. And she had managed to survive in a position of authority without making too many enemies, an admirable feat in the small town inside a small town that was Copeland. The girls didn't love Gerry, maybe, but they didn't hate her, either. In general she had their lukewarm respect. I badly needed a spokeswoman. Gerry would have to do.

With Claude distracted by the administrative demands of his post and Lou Davies busy with corporate legal matters, I was free to execute my battle plan as only I knew how. My high command in place, I dug a deep trench down the middle of the work force, ordering supervisors to cease all the informal socializing with the rank and file. It was an assault on the very playfulness that made work at Copeland bearable and an implied harbinger of things to come should Copeland be "unionized." I wanted supervisors and subordinates alike to wrestle with the irritations of an organizing drive every day and to hate the union for it.

"Your workers have declared war on you. And a war changes the rules we live by," I told the supervisors. I warned them that the union would use their friendships with workers as a weapon. They would twist an innocent social conversation between a supervisor and an employee into an accusation of spying or intimidation, and the unwitting supervisor would find herself dragged into court.

"Be careful of what you say and where you go and who you are with," I said. "In a union drive you can't trust anybody, not even your best friend. Just wait: you will see the nicest people turn into liars and thieves."

I allowed the morning housekeeping meetings to continue, for I thought them a useful forum for my purposes. I decided I could use the sessions to remind employees every day of how wonderful life at Copeland used to be before the union came along and screwed things up. The morning meetings were to go on, but without the joviality and spontaneity of the past, without the warmth. Kathleen was to keep things strictly business.

Otherwise, all social gatherings between ranks were verboten. I wanted to be sure the workers felt the tension of the union battle first thing in the morning. I told my troops they should not attend parties or baby showers or even go out to dinner with rank-and-file employees until the union election was behind us. For their own protection, I said. Anything could be a trap; anyone could be the bait. I even discouraged them from attending the Christmas festivities in their own departments.

The new rules came as a shock to supervisors, particularly the LPNs. To many Copeland employees, their co-workers had been like a second family. Most of the women led poor lives inside tiny houses in dull, small towns. Their greatest joy was coming to work, taking care of the old people, and spending the day with friends. They gossiped and giggled as they worked, they celebrated one another's birthdays, they sent flowers when a co-worker was sick. My rules put an end to all that, clouded the atmosphere, turned it dark and grim. Nurses were afraid to chat with their aides; aides and housekeepers fell silent when a nurse walked into the apartment in which they were working. Laundrywomen and waitresses could be seen ducking into elevators or scooting down the hall to avoid the inevitable, oppressive conversation with a supervisor. Friends stopped speaking.

After four weeks of counter-campaigning, the supervisors were beginning to break down. In that brief time they each had been forced to drop whatever they were doing several times a day to attend group brainwashing sessions or probing interviews with me. They had reported on their friends in exhaustive and embarrassing detail—to a stranger—and they had harangued those friends as well. Collectively the supervisors had made hundreds of individual letter deliveries, complete with the memorized explanations and probing questions and relentless follow-up that I ordered. In return they had been growled at, insulted, pushed aside, pleaded with, scolded, laughed at, cried to, and stonewalled. Many were having to skip lunch to get everything done, union-busting assignments on top of their regular duties, which were not lightened for the sake of the campaign. They were going home tense and angry, too upset to eat. They found themselves snapping at their husbands and yelling at their children and having a hard time getting to sleep at night. They were miserable. And it was only the beginning. There was so much more to come—more than even I knew.

During those first few weeks of the Copeland campaign, I had delivered my standard program; but all the while I was searching for a secret weapon and an Achilles' heel. Every company seemed to have one of each. At Copeland I found both in the old people, the heart and soul of the home. The Copeland employees loved those old people, every last one of them. Some of those old folks were cranky, some were ill, and some wouldn't talk at all. Nursing home work could be dirty, unpleasant, emotionally trying, sometimes demeaning. But for many workers, their relationships with the old men and women of Copeland transformed a mundane job into a vocation. Nurses, nurse's aides, housekeepers, cooks, waitresses, all of them, what they wanted most was to please the old people, to make their lives a little more comfortable. It didn't take much: a witty conversation, a special favor, a little time spent looking over pictures of great-grandchildren or admiring vintage jewelry. It brought the workers great joy to know that they were making the old people's lives just a little better, and it made them feel important. It was no accident that Copeland employees were so tender with the elderly residents; Claude had incorporated love and respect for the old people into every job description. When a worker was hired, even for the kitchen or the laundry room, she was told, "We are here for the residents. They pay your salary, and they are the most important part of your job. Talk to them. Take a little time out for them. Show them you care."

To me, those elderly residents were the "victims" I needed to make the union look truly evil. And I planned to use them. I figured that the Copeland organizing drive would not survive a threat on the old people. If I could convince the workers that the union would somehow jeopardize the well-being of the beloved residents, the pressure on union proponents would be unbearable. So, without saying a word to Lou Davies or Claude about my motives, I devised a dual strategy that totally subverted the Copeland mission.

First I blockaded the direct relationship between the line workers and the residents by imposing new formalities. Early on, I had Claude decree that "out of concern for the peace of mind of the residents," supervisors were to see to it that the old people were shielded from the hostilities of the organizing drive. They were not to be involved in any way. The supervisors were to make sure they would not be by prohibiting their subordinates from conversing or socializing with the residents. There would be no more lingering in the residents' rooms after a job was done, no dialogue except that which was necessary for the job. Lower-level employees would no longer be allowed to run errands or do special favors for the residents; if the residents needed something, the supervisors would be glad to get it for them. Workers were to stop addressing residents by their first name or nickname—as many of the old people preferred—and use only "Mr." or "Mrs." and the surname. It seemed a superficial change, but the new formality had a profound psychological impact. When "Dovie" became "Mrs. Jones," the old woman cried.

The official reason for these changes was to make sure the old people would not be manipulated or badgered by union people, used as propaganda tools. The real reason was that I wanted to manipulate them myself.

The sudden silence of their onetime confidantes made the old people nervous. They wondered to each other, "What next?" Naturally management blamed the new protocols on the union, explaining ever so patronizingly that the rules were being enforced for the residents' own protection. Protection? they wondered. Protection from what?

Once the seed was planted, the weed of fear just seemed to grow. It was easy to scare the old people into thinking that if the union got in, the residents would lose everything they held dear about their home at Copeland. Through my network I got the word out that life in a unionized nursing home would be Spartan and unpredictable. There would be pages and pages of regulations. There would be strikes, violence. What would happen to the old people while their caretakers were walking the picket line? The union would demand higher wages, and Copeland would have to raise its rates to pay salaries. What about the residents who couldn't afford to pay more? Where were they going to go? And what if worse came to worst and Copeland was forced to close its doors?

I didn't want to leave my propagandizing and fear-mongering to the shifting winds of rumor, however reliably those breezes had blown so far. I had a plan. It had come to my attention that there were a number of former corporate managers residing at Copeland, including a handful of retired CEOs. If I could get those savvy business types to bad-talk the union to their fellow residents—unofficially, of course, and spontaneously—I would be able to hit the workers from all sides. Every door the women opened as they went through their workday could lead them into another harangue or yet another plea. I mentioned to Claude that I would like to talk to some of his retired executives. He said he could do better. There was a residents committee at Copeland that met monthly to discuss matters of concern to the old people. Claude arranged for me to talk with the committee president, who happened to be a former management person; a few days later I met with a group of committee members. The committee agreed to send a letter to employees telling them they were afraid of what might happen to them if the union got in and asking them to please stop the union drive. I wrote the letter, the committee members signed it. From there the message of fear was spread to the entire residential community.

The old people's response was even more fiery than I had hoped. Several of them barked at the aides and housekeepers whenever they came into the apartment or harassed the kitchen help: "What the hell do you want a union for?" Others pleaded, "How could you do this to us?" Some even broke out weeping and fretted, "What if you go on strike? What's going to become of us?" Naturally Claude and Bill Hogg calmly assured the residents that they had no need to fear, that Copeland management would do everything in its power to keep them from harm. The message was clear: You folks have a damn good reason to be afraid, and the reason is the union.

As Christmas neared, life was becoming more and more unbearable around Copeland Oaks. My timing seemed perfect. I always liked to have the strife and dissension most intense around the holidays; it gave me great material. The union petition having been filed just after Thanksgiving, I had been cheated out of one of my favorite union-busting holidays. Thanksgiving, a time to be grateful for one's bounty, no matter how humble, was the perfect time for distribution of what I called my "count your blessings" letter. I considered that particular letter one of my masterpieces; it had always been a real crowd pleaser and astoundingly effective. I was not about to do without it at Copeland. So I recast the piece as a Christmas message. To ensure that the employees would accept the letter as sincere and spontaneous, I distributed it under the name of Gerry Sposato rather than Claude L. Roe. Written in a more fervent tone than the letters bearing Claude's signature, it was one of only two anti-union circulars in which I could replace Claude's rigid "Dear Staff Member" opening with my preferred, egalitarian greeting: "Dear Fellow Employee." No one would have taken the heartfelt plea seriously if it were said to spring from the impenetrable Dr. Roe. No, it was worker appealing to worker, sister to sister.

With my words, Gerry told her colleagues that the union had destroyed the loving working relationship among Copeland employees through a strategy of "divide and conquer." She charged union proponents with lying to workers about what the union could do for them and warned that the union might trade away the wonderful benefits of Copeland employment to which they had become accustomed. She repeated the charge that contract negotiation was nothing more than horse trading, and that the horse trading inevitably would require giving something back. The Christmas letter reinforced the continuing message that the union could guarantee nothing. It was true, in essence: in fact, the union would not be able to win a better life for Copeland workers unless the management agreed to give it. However, standing in the way of that better life was not some greedy union officer, but a gaggle of Copeland managers headed by Claude L. Roe.

107

Gerry's Christmas letter closed with a plea: "Christmas is a time to count our blessings, and I have attached to this letter a partial list of what would have to be put on a bargaining table and negotiated for if this union somehow becomes your bargaining agent."

The following page carried a typed list of twenty-six "blessings" and the implication that some or all could be lost in the collective bargaining process. The list ranged from such niceties as free meals and snacks; to protections that were required by law, such as workers' compensation insurance and disability pay; to inconsequential items like free parking—hardly a hot commodity in Sebring—and the availability of vending machines. Pay was not mentioned, nor were seniority rights, nor was health insurance, nor was respect, nor was consistency, nor was fairness, nor were working conditions, which were the actual issues on which the organizing drive turned.

At the foot of the page was a cartoon I had clipped from the local newspaper, then altered to reinforce the idea in a humorous way. The cartoon pictured a smug-looking Santa Claus, arms crossed in front of him, with a little boy seated in his lap. The boy was handing Santa a pencil and a piece of paper bearing the initials IOU. Santa, his eyes closed in an indication of intransigence, was saying, "I'll do my best kid . . . but I'm not signing anything." On Santa's hat I had penciled in "SEIU #47." Below the cartoon I had written an emphatic "Vote No!"

The letter was distributed on Christmas Eve. Unbeknownst to Claude, a few days later, while a bedraggled Christmas spirit still lingered in the frosty air, I dispatched a contingent of commandos to scratch up the cars of high-profile pro-company workers and to make threatening phone calls to others. I bade farewell to 1980 with a letter from Claude taking the union to task for such barbarous scare tactics.

I could not know yet that my anti-union campaign at Copeland would go on for a full year and a half. All that time, while purportedly saving Copeland money, Claude paid me more than $15,000 a month. It would take a Copeland housekeeper two years of sheet changing and bathroom scrubbing to earn that much money. But the employees would never know about that. And that number doesn't count the perquisites like free meals, mileage expenses, and, toward the end of the campaign, a free room, which cost Copeland $1,000 a month in lost income. Nor does it count the thousands of dollars in attorneys' fees. The employees would never know about that.

Alice came to work in mid-January, at a rate of $500 a day.

By that time I had figured out which supervisors would work for me and which ones I could brand as "useless"—at least I thought I had. Into the useless category I lumped two types of supervisors: those who clearly sympathized with their workers' organizing effort and those who, without knowing it, had such little credibility with their subordinates that it would be foolish of me to allow them to carry the company message. I knew from training and experience, however, that I could not simply ignore those supervisors, no matter how little use they were to me, particularly that second group. If I were to slight them, they might turn on me and, one never knew, maybe even develop a following among an ego-bruised middle-management corps. Yet as a one-man band I had many much more crucial parts to play than theirs and didn't want to waste my time nurturing their delusions. Whenever there were several consultants on a job, we simply traded off the distasteful task of meeting with the pests. But at Copeland I was alone. How was I going to finesse this? Then I got a brilliant idea: I would dump the pests on Alice.

Of course, I never phrased it in that way, but that is essentially what I did. I set Alice up in a sort of shell campaign that paralleled mine and began funneling half a dozen benign but "useless" supervisors into long daily interviews with her. I didn't care what the supervisors said during their hours with Alice, and I didn't much care what she told them. I just wanted them to talk and talk and feel that we were listening. In that way I yanked everyone I didn't want to bother with out of the campaign without them even knowing it.

I introduced Alice to the supervisors during the first meeting of the New Year 1981. Admonishing my audience to give her the same respect they gave me, I told the crowd she was not only my wife, but my partner, and said we would be working the remainder of the campaign together until the election, the date of which, by the way, still had not been set.

Alice managed a sweet smile and a soft "Hello" to the crowd, but she was feeling faint. She had been a nervous wreck during the drive to Sebring and had tried to talk me out of using her. She wouldn't know what to say, she told me. What if they asked her questions she couldn't answer? She didn't know anything about unions; she couldn't think on her feet the way I could, and she knew it.

What Alice didn't know was that none of that mattered. I hadn't dared tell my dear wife the true plan. I had told her the same story I had told Claude: that some of the workers might feel more comfortable talking to a woman, and that she was a natural. For the ruse to work, I needed Alice to be wholly genuine in the interviews. I needed her to console and commiserate and cry with true empathy. Alice being a guileless lady, she would have been incapable of pulling off the job if she had known it was a hoax.

"Alice," I said, "don't worry. You'll be great."

And in fact, she was. One of the first supervisors to have a session with Alice was Kathleen; she, like several others, bonded with my wife in a way she never had with me. My wife's sessions were filled with tears and hugs and heartfelt words of encouragement. Everybody felt better; nobody got in the way.

With the useless supes off the road, I had more room to maneuver with my special forces. Usually I counted on a handful of elite warriors to carry the campaign for the ineffective supervisors. But at Copeland all I needed was Judy Stanley. Judy was the resident social worker at Copeland, a plump, plain-faced twenty-nine-year-old from the nearby Quaker town of Beloit. She was more highly educated than most of her co-workers, having received her bachelor's degree in psychology as well as a license in social work. She fancied herself a real pro with people and aspired to a position of authority within the Copeland organization. Judy admired me. She was intrigued by my keen, totally intuitive lock on human psychology. And she was loyal like a puppy. Judy was single, homely, and—I thought at the time—destined to be a spinster forever. Copeland was her family and her life. Her job meant everything to her, and she would do anything if she were convinced it was for the good of the home. Helping me shoot down this union, I convinced her, was the best thing we could do.

I took Judy under my wing, and I turned her into a one-woman SWAT team. I taught her, trained her, molded her into a perfect little soldier. In her job as social worker, Judy roamed the Copeland complex, meeting with residents to help them untangle upsetting problems, which usually involved some intimidating government bureaucracy like the Social Security Administration or the IRS. She set her own daily schedule, and she knew just about everyone. As soon as she knew the rhetoric and the false logic of my campaign, I commissioned her as the mine sweeper. She followed the tracks of the less able supervisors, reinforcing my antiunion message—emphasis on my the-union-will-tear-us-apart theme—delivering the promise of harmony and making a plea for another chance. People listened to Judy, it seemed; she was articulate, she was sincere.

Judy bought into my program so eagerly, believed the ruse so completely, that I was almost sorry for her.

On January 19 the NLRB finally decided that it did, in fact, have jurisdiction over Copeland, and the workers had a right to hold a representation election. The board set the election for one month later, February 19. Then, and only then, was the union entitled to get the Excelsior list—my severely edited version, of course. After five months of work, then, and only then, were organizers able to find out the names and addresses of everyone in the voting unit. Then, and only then, would the union have the chance to contact all the workers. I had my offensive ready: the same letter that informed the workers of the time and place of the upcoming election also warned them to expect intrusions from a desperate and bothersome union.

Election day began at 6:30 A.M.

Snow covered the ground.

The sky was still dark when the NLRB agent arrived about a half hour before the voting was to begin. Claude greeted him at the big white doors, showed him into the Williamsburg Lounge, and disappeared into his office; management was not allowed near the polling place during voting hours. In the lounge, the agent was joined by the designated election observers—half a dozen pro-union workers and half a dozen management people—who would make it their job to be sure nothing slippery occurred during the balloting. The two contingents huddled on opposite sides of the room, whispered, peered over at the enemy. Then the agent called their attention. He was about to perform the legally required ballot box ritual that I always referred to as the "magic act."

The agent stood behind an oak table, and the observers assembled before it. He picked up what looked like a thin pile of brown cardboard sheets and, with a flick of his arm—pop!—flipped the pile into the form of a two-foot-long rectangular tunnel. The agent held the tunnel straight out at the level of his chest, allowing observers to look through it straight to his gray suit. Without saying a word, he solemnly passed a fisted hand through the space. Keeping the tunnel parallel to the floor, he moved it in a slow half circle, parading its emptiness before everyone in the room. That accomplished, the agent turned the tunnel vertically and quickly folded the lower ends upward to create a bottom. He turned the box on its side and showed it to the observers once again, proving to the suspicious that there was still nothing inside. Setting the box on the table, he then folded down four upper panels, making a slotted top.

The agent checked his watch. A line had formed at the doorway. With ten minutes to go, he set up the portable voting booth at one end of the room. He instructed one observer from each camp to take a seat on either side of him at the table. He took out his copy of the Excelsior list, which he would check to be sure no one voted twice. The rest of the observers stationed themselves about the lounge. At 6:30 sharp the agent let the voting begin.

I stayed with Claude in his office throughout the morning vote, listening to him identify wild-bird calls on an Audubon Society recording. At 8:00 A.M. the polls closed; they would reopen again at 2:30 P.M., half an hour before the afternoon shift was to begin. When the morning session ended, the agent sealed the ballot box as prescribed by law, taping the edges and corners and having the observers sign the tape. Then everyone left the room.

When I wandered into the lounge a little later, I was surprised to find the box sitting unattended on the top of the oak table. The agents usually take the box with them wherever they go, even to the rest room. I looked at it, looked around the empty room, looked behind me at the closed door. It would be easy, I thought. I wouldn't have to stuff the box; all I would have to do is make it clear the box had been tampered with, and the election would be held invalid. Then the union would have to go through the organizing drive all over again. I would blame the union for whatever I did to the box, which would give me the added ammunition of the union's obvious criminality.

I milled around the room, pacing like a tiger. I had called the election a winner, and for that reason I couldn't decide whether it would be worth the risk. My internal struggle was interrupted by a very flustered board agent, who came racing back into the room, his face flushed. I was nowhere near the box.

The second voting time ended at 4:00 P.M., just as the sky outside was beginning to darken. It had been a long, tense day. Supervisors were even more on edge than their workers. For the voters, election day held hope and promise, even after all that had been done to them. Not so for the supervisors. For them it was the moment of truth, the day they would discover if they were still despised, as they must have been when their workers called in the union. It was the day they would learn whether their coworkers were their enemies or their friends. Of the dozens of employees who showed up for the vote count, most were supervisors. They, all of them, needed to see it through to the end. Those on the morning shift didn't go home—they grouped in the Williamsburg Lounge. Afternoon workers stopped by on their breaks or wandered through on their way to care for a patient. Out in the hallways there was nothing but silence.

The agent took his seat behind the oak table, flanked by an observer from each side. He punched the seal, tore open the ballot box, and began to count. One by one he unfolded the ballots and read them aloud; one by one the observers marked "yes" or "no" on their tally sheet. At first, each call provoked a gasp from one side of the room, a muffled cheer from the other. But as the count progressed, the room fell silent. It was too close.

When the last ballot had been counted, the agent announced the results. The room erupted.

"Oh, my God," someone exclaimed.

"All right!" cheered someone else.

Judy's eyes filled. Kathleen covered her face. A trio of nurses wept aloud. Across the room, another group of girls squealed and wrapped their arms around each other. "Hey, we got 'em!" a voice proclaimed. A sharp hoot ripped through the room. A couple of girls dashed out the door. Suddenly there was clapping and cheering breaking out all over Copeland.

The union had won.

(But keep reading to find out what **really** happened—The Editor)

Did you notice the constant pressure, the overwhelming effort that went into this campaign?

The constant barrage of communication from the company?

Designed to drown the union in questions from members?

Keep them constantly on the defensive?

How important was solidarity in this chapter?

Do you see parallels in the methods used in this chapter and our challenges?

Do you think our union could sustain our fight against the limitless money spent by the company in a campaign like this?

A page from the Editor

When you deal with union busting, even 'winning' may not count.

This section continues to follow the efforts at Copeland Oaks.

How does this apply to us?

Do you wonder why negotiations take so long?

Do you think the company is 'bargaining in good faith'?

This section will open your eyes to the reality we face today.

And don't forget the QR code links to the author's words from the period where he worked to right the wrongs he had done for so many years.

The Editor

Bloodletting

Claude didn't blame me.

Still, I was sorry. If I had thought there was even a chance we might lose, I would have told him. Just good business. The only kind of surprise I liked was a win much bigger than the one I had predicted. This way it was embarrassing. True, we lost by only five votes, but I hadn't expected it to be anywhere near that close. Every pro-company employee had voted; I had made sure of that. So where had I gone wrong? I was dumbfounded. I never mentioned it to Claude, but I kept thinking about that unguarded ballot box, about how I could have taken care of things right there.

On election night Claude and his wife invited me and Alice out to dinner. What a good sport, I thought. Many CEOs might have snarled, "Thanks for nothing," and slammed the door in my face. But not Claude. Claude bought me steak and wine, and we spent a good long time licking our wounds together at the finest restaurant in Alliance.

"I was buffaloed," I confessed to Claude as we took our first sips of Cabernet. "I really believed I had it counted right. All I can figure is, an awful lot of the girls must have been lying. I'll bet it was the nurses."

I had lost before—not a lot, three or four times, maybe—but never without realizing it in advance, never without having the chance to prepare my client. It felt terrible. I apologized to Claude a dozen times; he absolved me many times over. What a good sport.

We made small talk about other details of my life: the brick house Alice and I had rented in the old University Heights district of Cleveland; the Jewish day care and private elementary school we had found for the boys in order to evade the urban public schools; how hard it had been for Alice to share the castle with my mom during the weeks we all had lived together in Beachwood. But the conversation always wound its way back to the election, to the union, to what went wrong. Claude was conciliatory.

"It was a great campaign, Marty," he said. "I wouldn't have wanted you to do anything differently. In fact, if you're willing, I'd like you to stick around for a while and work with the supervisors."

It seemed that Claude was taking the high road, accepting that the union had beat him and going on. He would have me run monthly workshops to teach the supervisors how to handle the union, keep tabs on the grapevine maybe through a rotating roundtable, and let it go. Could it be? Hardly. By the time the waiter was grinding black pepper onto my tossed green salad, I realized that old Claude was not a good sport at all. He hadn't said it yet, but I knew that as far as he was concerned, he hadn't lost. This thing wasn't over; it had only just begun.

I agreed to come in the next morning to meet with Claude and Lou Davies, and when I arrived, Davies was already there. Claude was seated behind his desk, looking grave. This time there was no small talk, no merriment. Barely had the door shut behind me when Claude announced in a solemn voice that there was not to be a contract at Copeland Oaks. He turned to the attorney and commanded him to be Copeland's representative at the bargaining table.

Lou leaned forward on the chair he occupied facing Claude's desk. He looked into Claude's cold eyes, shook his head slowly, and refused. "I can't do it, Claude," he said, almost whispering. "I know you don't intend to bargain in good faith. For me to go to the bargaining table with no intention of reaching a contract would be unethical. It's called surface bargaining, and it's against my professional code of conduct."

Claude frowned. He hadn't counted on that. He sat silently for a moment; then a smile flickered across his lips. He turned to me.

I knew instinctively what he was thinking, and I nodded in agreement. But, of course: unlike Lou, I was not bound by any code of ethics or any professional canons and therefore would not have to worry about my behavior at the bargaining table. In fact, for the purposes of my resume, the naughtier I was, the better. The worst thing that could happen if I got caught surface bargaining was that the NLRB would order Copeland to bargain in good faith. And even the good-faith order was unlikely, because a charge of surface bargaining is very difficult to substantiate. The union people would need witnesses; I would have as many as they. The union people would need documentation; that would be hard to come by if nothing was happening. All I would have to do to defend myself would be to show that I had agreed to something, that some progress had been made. The law imposes on management and a newly elected union a "duty to bargain" for twelve months, and no more. I figured I could jerk off the union for a year, no problem. I told Claude I'd be glad to do it.

Claude also wanted me to go ahead with the supervisor training and the employee discussion groups as I had planned, in preparation for Copeland's certain return to monarchy. That was fine with me. For one thing, it meant one more day each month that I would pocket $750; that was on top of my daily fee for handling the negotiations. What's more, the supervisor meetings would give me the perfect forum for spreading my version of what was happening at the bargaining table and other important lies.

I called the first meeting immediately; I wanted to seize upon the intense emotions aroused by the company's humiliating loss. Many of the supervisors were shaken by the pro-union vote, as if it were a personal tragedy. I had taught them well. They were in anguish. They felt betrayed. They were hurt, confused, angry. But for the moment the targets of their passion were many: many of the women were as angry at Copeland and at Claude and at me as they were at the employees and their union. If I was to revive the anti-union drive from its startling knock-out, I had to collect all that rancor and aim it squarely at the workers who dealt the blows. And I had to do it quickly, before the supervisors could come to consider that life in an organized company might not be so bad.

Two days after the big upset election one hundred dispirited nurses, secretaries, and department managers assembled in the Williamsburg Lounge. No one spoke. Some still wore the telltale puffy eyes and red noses of a long crying spell. Others were pale and walked with a hypnotic stare. They looked beaten, dejected. Looking out at the faces of my grief-stricken troops, I realized that many expected to be scolded. They would not be. I did not want them contrite, not now. I wanted them angry.

The days of the this-is-all-your-fault tack and the give-us-a-chance tack were behind us. I would have no use in the post-election campaign for the soft emotions. There would be no more begging and pleading, no apologizing, no wooing. Now there would be nothing but fire.

So I told them, in steady, modulated tones, "Ladies, I know this is a very trying time for most of you. You have worked hard, and I have to say, you did one fantastic job. Truly. So, hold your heads high. You have nothing to be ashamed of. The only people who should be ashamed are the traitors who voted against their company. After all you did these past three months, listening to them and talking with them and trying your level best to make your company a better place, those creeps went right ahead and stabbed you in the back. They lied to you. They told you they were your friends, then they turned around and voted against you anyway. Well, now they're going to pay. We will show them that we spoke the truth in the campaign. And they'll see they made a terrible mistake. They wanted a union, let's give them a union."

Already the mood had shifted. The meeting room was abuzz. Nurses began whispering to each other, quite a few were smiling, some were even chuckling. With a lighter touch to my voice now, I reminded the supervisors that all the union had won was twelve months, nothing more. It had not won a contract. "We have lost the battle," I said, "but we have not yet lost the war."

The negotiation of a first contract is very delicate, so the process is highly controlled by labor law. Company executives who have just been forced to recognize a union—after spending tens of thousands of dollars to defeat it—rarely walk into their first bargaining session with open arms. To protect the inchoate contract from sabotage by an embittered management, then, labor law sets rigid rules of conduct for the postelection period. The purpose of the rules is to impede management from undermining negotiations, whether through subtle bribes, veiled threats, or an outright propaganda campaign. As with most labor laws, however, the rules are largely ineffective. Worse: the hands of a union buster can quite easily twist those rules into a precision weapon against the union.

During the post-electoral battle, I would not be able to send letters to the rank-and-file employees as I had during the counter-organizing campaign. Any memo or letter coming from management that even hinted at criticizing the union could be interpreted by the labor board as an attempt to undermine the union and negotiations. That would make the company look like the bad guy— which I didn't want—and could pressure Claude into actually negotiating, which he did not want. There was nothing, however, to stop us from talking to the supervisors. We would continue our propaganda war all right, we just wouldn't put it in writing. Once again the supervisors were taken hostage.

I looked out at my audience. It was hungry. Hundreds of eyes were upon me, begging me for relief from pain and emptiness. I began the feeding, slowly at first, then picking up the pace as my captives became accustomed to their new meal. In one hour I had to whip every vestige of remorse and forgiveness out of all those loving hearts and refill the empty space with spite. Labor law was going to help me accomplish my aim. All I had to do was take every rule that suited my game plan and stretch it to the extreme. I would ignore the spirit and enforce the letter of the law so far beyond its intent that it would double back on itself and end up destroying the very process—and the very people—it was written to protect.

My strategy was predetermined by the campaign that had just ended. Throughout three months of war I had made many a horrifying prediction of what could happen to Copeland should the union win the election. Now I would make sure that every last one of the dire forecasts came to pass. I had warned that the cherished "direct relationship" between supervisor and worker would come to an end. I had warned that the two sides would see each other, and treat each other, as enemies. I had warned that all flexibility in scheduling, in duties, in everything, would disappear. I had warned that negotiations could be prolonged and uncertain. I had warned that Copeland would stagnate during those negotiations; there would be no workplace improvements, no pay raises. And I had warned that there could be a strike, that there might be violence that the residents would be in jeopardy. Now it was time to deliver.

"I can't imagine that many of you have been in the army," I quipped to my audience, looking the younger ones in the eyes. I knew them all so well, now. I smiled, and the levity was received with gratitude. "It doesn't matter," I said, chuckling. "You don't need to have been in the army to know about drill instructors. How many of you know what a drill instructor is?" Hands shot up around the room. I let a sly smile rest on my lips. "Good. I thought so. Well, that's what I want you all to become. Starting today, you are drill instructors. Shore up your departments. You are the bosses, you make the rules, and you keep everyone in line. It's clear to me—and it should be clear to you—that you can't trust your workers. You were lied to, you were betrayed, and you can't know for certain who did the lying and the betraying. So everybody gets the tough treatment.

"The employees wanted the structure of a union," I continued. "That's what that vote was all about. Well, we'll show them how it works. Flexibility will disappear. There will be no give and take, no favors, no compassion, no bending of rules."

I decreed that supervisors were not to talk to any subordinates—at all—except to give orders. Any personal ties to their employees that had

121

survived the organizing campaign were to be severed immediately. "From now on, there's no room for understanding. Everything," I said, "everything will be done by the book."

Funny thing was, until I appeared at Copeland, there was no book. Claude had never bothered to put employment policies in writing—indeed, in many areas there were no actual policies. At my insistence, during the previous months, Claude and his helpmates had thrown together a handbook that spelled out the mundane details of Copeland employment, such as work hours and duties, discipline procedures, management rights and responsibilities, and absentee policies. Where rules and procedures did not exist, something was made up on the spot for the benefit of the handbook. The policies were then typed up on looseleaf sheets and collected in a three-ring binder—a precaution that I routinely recommended so that management could rewrite any policy in a moment. Now, suddenly, this hastily prepared shell manual was to become the bible.

Claude declined to include in the manual a number of niceties, preferring to think of them as unearned perquisites to be doled out and taken away at his whim. I took some favorites away immediately. The first to go was the morning and afternoon breaks, two coveted fifteen-minute respites from the daily tedium. Gone. No more idleness at company expense. Then went free meals, a real blow to the workers. Technically such changes could be illegal, if the purpose of the changes was to undermine the union. Labor law recognizes the elected union as the sole and exclusive bargaining agent for wages, hours, benefits, and working conditions and encourages management to maintain everything in those areas at status quo until a contract is agreed to and signed by both sides. My answer to that was: So what? If the union wanted to file a complaint about the changes, fine, let the labor board decide. In the meantime the changes would go into effect.

Where the status quo guidelines did not suit me, I ignored them. Where they did suit my purpose, however, I made sure they were enforced with a vengeance. In the area of pay, benefits, and working conditions, Copeland employees hungered for improvements. All Claude would have had to do to grant a pay raise while negotiations with Local 47 were in process was get the union's okay. The union might have hated to let management take the credit for a pay increase, but it would hardly have been able to refuse. The new members would never have understood. Same thing for any other improvement, from upgrading medical insurance to fixing toilets. Management had only to ask. Well, Claude was not about to ask the union for anything, and I wouldn't have let him if he had been so inclined. No, the workers were just going to have to wait and curse the union as they tightened their belts. A de facto wage freeze had gone into effect at Copeland three months earlier, the day the union had filed its petition. But because raises at Copeland were sporadic and minuscule at best, the action—or, more accurately, inaction—went largely unnoticed. That was to change. After the union vote, Claude extended the freeze indefinitely.

We had the supervisors make a lot of noise about the lack of pay raises. The noise went something like this: "Copeland Oaks would like to give everybody a raise; in fact, a raise had been considered for this month. But the federal government says we can't raise wages as long as negotiations are pending." Then, the personal touch: "I know you need the money, Nan. But there's nothing we can do about it. Our hands are tied—by the union."

My final order to the troops on that first day of phase II was that they be particularly rigid with the known "troublemakers" who had gotten everybody into this mess in the first place. Also referred to as the "red-hots," those union pushers were bad seeds, I said. They were not to be left alone for a moment, lest they breed even more misery. "Bird-dog them," I ordered. "Wherever a troublemaker goes, a supervisor must go, too; into the ladies' room, down to the lockers, to the dining room, out on the grounds, into a resident's apartment. A troublemaker must never have a chance to talk privately with other workers, and she must never, ever, be left alone with one of the old folks. We can't take that chance. No telling what she might do." The union couldn't do much about all that, for their role now was limited to bargaining. The only right they had won was the right to try to negotiate a contract.

As I revived the ground war, I also recast the war of delay. This time the delay revolved not around the hearing room of the NLRB, but around the bargaining table. As word of the wage freeze and evidence of the new military order spread throughout Copeland Oaks, so did the message that, so far, the union had done nothing. In fact, union officers were busy drawing up a proposed contract. But they had not contacted Copeland and clearly felt no pressure to move quickly. Why should they? After all, they had no idea they were still at war. They thought they had won. I did not call the union, nor did Claude. We just went about unfolding our in-house drama and waited for the union to come to us. They only had twelve months, and the clock was ticking. We were in no rush. Time was on our side.

Six weeks after the election, Claude got a letter from the union attorney asking the executive director to schedule the first bargaining session. Claude wrote back saying that all future correspondence should be sent to his representative, Martin Jay Levitt; he gave my home address and telephone number. Since I was required at Copeland only two half days a month then, I had resumed my kitchen table routine. Eventually I found a handful of other union-busting jobs to keep me busy, but for the first couple of months after the Copeland election I spent most of my days at home drinking and just passing the time.

In mid-April 1981, about a month after Claude had received the union letter, I got a call from Local 47. "We need to start negotiations," said the voice at the other end of the line. "Can we meet out at Copeland Oaks? It's gonna be tough for our committee to get all the way up here to Cleveland."

Instinctively I said no. Why? Partly because I didn't feel like driving out to Sebring and partly just to make things difficult on the union members. "Dr. Roe doesn't want any bargaining to take place at his facility," I lied. "It might be upsetting to the residents."

In that case, said the union man, we could use the conference room at union headquarters in downtown Cleveland. He mentioned matter-of-factly that the members of his negotiating committee would naturally need paid time off in order to attend negotiations.

"I'm sure my client will have no trouble granting time off," said I, "but I can also assure you it won't be paid."

I had some demands of my own. I told the union man that I required Joe Murphy, president of Local 47, to be present at every bargaining session. "I'm not interested in bargaining with anyone less than the president of the local," I said.

The voice answered, "That's going to be very difficult. Mr. Murphy has a very busy schedule."

I retorted, "Well, so do I." Pretending to check that schedule, I then told my union contact that the first date I had available was in two weeks. We set the meeting for 4:30 P.M. on a Wednesday. Before hanging up, I said I needed the names of every employee on the negotiating team so that I could arrange time off for the meeting. For most of the workers, that wasn't going to be necessary, I knew. I had been careful to schedule the session after the end of the day shift, to make it a hardship for the workers, some of whom surely would have to get back to their families. The real reason for obtaining the names was to give me time to arrange for the immediate supervisor of each committee member to be present at negotiations.

By the time I met Jim Horton, Art Worthy, and Joe Murphy face to face, two months had passed. Two down, ten to go.

I walked into the first session twenty minutes late and as blustery as ever. Behind me were six stern-faced supervisors. I had instructed the bosses to take the seat directly across from their subordinate, if possible, then to keep quiet. They thought they had been invited along to observe the proceedings so that they could report the facts to their crews. In truth they were there only to intimidate. I told them nothing about negotiations, nothing. When Kathleen Taylor walked in, the face of one committee member fell. Then in walked Anna Moracco, director of nursing, and I saw another face grow pale.

I took my seat. Jim Horton introduced himself; the union attorney, Mel Swartzwall; and Joe Murphy. The attorney handed me a typed list of demands. He asked, "Do you have anything in writing?"

I didn't. I growled, "It's not my obligation to bring something in writing to you. That's your job."
The union people remained unruffled, but everyone else in the room shifted on their seats and glanced at one another uneasily. Not about to waste precious bargaining time, the attorney suggested, "Well, since we're here, let's get some routine things out of the way. We'd like union shop and check-off—"

I stopped him there. The union was asking Copeland to agree to require all employees to pay union dues and to deduct those dues automatically from paychecks. "Wait a minute," I told him. "We're not prepared to consider that yet. Remember, this was a close election." I decided to keep the meeting short, a show of how futile bargaining could be and to frustrate all those inconvenienced people. Saying I needed to review the union proposals before I could proceed, I suggested we call it a day.

The union contingent was eager to set the next meeting time. I was not. I said my calendar was jammed, and that I'd have to look it over and get back to them. I then reissued my demand that Murphy attend every bargaining session. The entire union side of the table protested; having to work meetings around Joe's packed schedule was going to bog things down. But I insisted: this being a first contract, it was of utmost importance that the president of the local be involved. I unilaterally adjourned the session, rose, and told the union I'd be in touch by telephone. My contingent of supervisors stood and exited behind me.

I called a supervisors meeting at Copeland the next day. I wanted to be sure I got my story out on the wire before the union had a chance to deliver its version. "We'll be first with the facts," I had told the supervisors, and I was holding true to my promise. There was little to report, I said. I told my audience about a gruff, sour union president who, now that he had won the election, didn't want to do the work of negotiating. I told them about the predictable demand for union shop and check-off but said nothing about the twenty-four-page, detailed proposal the union had prepared for that first bargaining session. In fact, I never even read the proposal. I had no idea what they were asking for, didn't need to know. I had no intention of ever talking about it.

I didn't call the union back as I had said I would. Two weeks passed, and Jim Horton called me. I was brusque. "I've been busy," I snapped.

The union wanted to schedule the next meeting as soon as possible; Horton wanted to know if we could meet at Copeland Oaks this time. Out of the question, I said.

"It's a hardship on those working people to travel up to Cleveland," he protested.

I agreed to consider an alternate place but left it up to him to come up with one. We left it at that.

Jim Horton called me back a little while later with the name of a roadside motel fifteen minutes outside of Sebring. We could use the meeting room there, he said. Now, let's set a date. He suggested the following Tuesday; I reminded him that I expected Joe Murphy to be there.

"Mr. Murphy's not available on that day," he replied, "but we're ready to go."

I balked. "If he's not available, then I'm not available."

We finally agreed on a date two weeks later. Before signing off, Horton reminded me, "Oh, and Marty, bring a counterproposal this time. Something in writing."

"I'll see what I can do," was all I would say.

When I walked into the second session with my team, the union people were a bit more aggressive but still terribly polite. They asked for my counterproposal immediately. I said no, I did not have a proposal ready; but in the next breath I assured them I was prepared to negotiate. To keep the talks going and create a patina of "good faith," I agreed to a handful of routine items. In negotiating lingo, I "initialed off" on a series of penny items such as recognition of the union, equal opportunity employment, and the like by scrawling my initials alongside the sections. It was a cursory gesture, which took care of but one page of the union's twenty-five-page proposal. It meant nothing, but it bought me some time and created evidence that I was, in fact, willing to negotiate. The process took all of five minutes, at the end of which there was nothing left to do, since I had not yet responded to the proposal handed me a month earlier. The union people looked perturbed. Swartzwall began to grumble. Then Murphy took over, waxing genteel before his newly won members and their bosses.

"Come on, Marty," he cajoled. "You know we need a written proposal from you if we're going to get anywhere. What do you say?"

I feigned cooperation, saying in a mellifluous voice, "I'll do what I can to put something together." We set the next session for two weeks thence, same place. I let the union pick up the tab for the room.

The following meeting was like a gift sent from the great Union Buster below. Naturally I brought not a scrap of paper with me. But the other side would never know that. When I entered the meeting room—late, as usual—I noticed Joe Murphy was not present. After the management people and I had taken our seats, I called the oversight to the union's attention.

Horton responded apologetically, "Mr. Murphy had a last-minute conflict and regrets that he cannot attend today's session."

That did it. They had handed me my bluff. "What?" I boomed, full of indignation. "We had an agreement!"

The union attorney told me to shut up, the other committee members tried to be more conciliatory, but I wasn't letting go. With the help of Lou Davies I had boned up on the myriad ways in which unions protected their right to represent workers, just in case I was forced into a bargaining session; I had planned to waste that day arguing over the technicalities of union membership. But this was better.

I jumped up from my seat and bellowed, "If your top man can't bother to be here, I'm not wasting my time." I turned to my stunned committee and announced, "We have nothing more to discuss." On cue, my troops rose with me, and we all marched out of the room, leaving the union team in shocked silence.

Four down, eight to go.

Back at Copeland my war machine was steamrolling along. I met with supervisors regularly in order to add a few strokes to the portrait I was painting in their minds, the portrait of an inept, uncaring, and potentially dangerous union. Under the blessed banner of "communication" I reported on the pathetic bargaining sessions, I floated rumors, spread fear. I also spent one morning a month with supervisors delivering my training program. The class plans were simple: one thirty-minute canned film on responsive management or positive reinforcement or the team approach or some other overblown management concept, followed by an apparently freewheeling discussion, which, on the heels of the film and in the context of the continuing anti-union drive, was quite easy to guide toward certain desired conclusions. So straightforward was the system that a trainer was barely needed, except to run the projector and keep the talk from falling off the track.

After a few sessions I began handing the work over to Judy Stanley, whom I was grooming to carry on for me when my job at Copeland was done. Most of the information in the training films as well as the ideas circulated during discussions could be considered harmless. Some might even have been useful, had they not been tainted by the narrow and belligerent motive of keeping the workers unorganized and under control.

On a separate morning each month, I had Judy conduct the rotating roundtable discussions with rank-and-file workers. Since I was acting as negotiator for Copeland, I still chose not to speak with employees directly. It was to my strategic advantage that the rap sessions were moderated by a lowbrow middle manager like Judy, who, although classified as a supervisor, was nobody's direct boss and was not seen as a threat. The workers would open up to her, I figured; at the very least they would not be afraid to open up to each other in front of her. I sent Judy into each meeting with a tightly choreographed program designed to make workers feel good by letting them voice their complaints and to squeeze intelligence out of the fecund employee grapevine. At the start of the discussion, which was attended each time by a different worker representative from each department, Judy assured the group that whatever they said would be held in strictest confidence. Although she might need to report what was said so that management could accomplish the improvements the workers sought, she would never, ever, divulge the source of any complaint. Any notes she took would be totally anonymous. She promised, and she meant it. After each session, when Judy reported to me not only every detail of the discussion, but the names of her sources, she never imagined that I would break her trust and use the information against the employees.

Out on the floor, the atmosphere was even more oppressive than during the organizing effort. "After the union passed, that's when they blasted us," remembers former housekeeper Jean Householder. Jean was a prominent and fearless union supporter. A onetime friend of her boss, Kathleen Taylor, Jean ran the organizing drive in the housekeeping and laundry departments. A thirty-nine-year-old with twelve years at Copeland, she was an election observer and a member of the negotiating committee. She was also one of the chief targets of Copeland's post-electoral bloodbath. I saw Jean, and about twenty-three other key union proponents, as the biggest impediment to my campaign to discredit the newly elected union. Those two dozen women were keeping workers informed almost as well as I was; they could be counted on both to rebut my disinformation and to inspire nerve-racked employees to stick with the union. I figured that if I could get them out of the way over the next few months, while maintaining the unofficial impasse at the bargaining table, I just might be able to fuel a worker revolt against the union.

I knew, and Claude confirmed, that employee turnover in nursing homes was quite high. Nine, ten months from now, as much as one-third of Copeland employees could be new hires. They would not have voted in the representation election, and they would have been hired in part for their verifiable anti-union inclinations. With no strong union leaders left at the job, a union decertification campaign could spread quickly.

Claude bought off a handful of the former union activists right away, through minor promotions. But what I really wanted was for Jean and her pals to quit. To that end, I made sure they could not enjoy one minute of their workday, the pressure on them and the hostility toward them would be so intense. Supervisors, coworkers, and residents would gang up on the remaining twenty and blame them for everyone's unhappiness. The target twenty would draw lousy shifts and find themselves with the most despised assignments; they would be harassed, shunned, and punished until life at Copeland became so unbearable that they would decide they owed it to themselves—and to their loving families—to find another job. If that didn't work, of course, they would have to be fired.

The Jean plan was boilerplate harassment, but it was nonetheless effective for its lack of originality. A harassed worker feels totally alone, no matter how many tens of thousands of workers have been similarly harassed, in a different time, at a different place. Immediately following the union win, Jean was paired with her direct supervisor, the assistant director of housekeeping and laundry, Betty Rusky. The pairing had a double aim: one, of course, was to subject Jean to the constant hostility of her ego-injured boss. The other was to underhandedly double Jean's workload. Since Betty was constantly being pulled off the floor for meetings—with me, with the department heads, with upper management—Jean was constantly having to clean their twelve rooms and change the linens in twelve others with no help. When they were together, Jean and Betty labored in tense silence. One morning, on one of the rare occasions Jean was cleaning an apartment alongside her boss-partner, she believes she overheard the elderly resident whisper to Betty, "What about these union people they're telling us about? They say we're supposed to lock our doors against them at night." Betty put her index finger to her lips, glanced over at Jean, and whispered back, "Shhhhh. She goes to negotiations with them."

After a few months Jean could take no more. In March 1982 she quit her job.

Sharing the bull's-eye with the twenty "red-hot" Copeland women was one man—in fact, a supervisor, Fred Moracco. Fred, a big-bellied fellow nearing sixty, was the director of maintenance and husband of Anna Moracco, the nursing director. Fred knew Copeland Oaks better than Claude, better than anyone. Heck, he had built the place. When Copeland was under construction in the mid-1960s, Fred had been the project foreman—and the union steward. A union laborer since the 1940s, Fred quit construction work and left the International Laborers Union in 1968 to take the job as Copeland's head maintenance man. With that move, he forfeited the pension he had been building with the union at ten cents an hour for twenty-five years. But that was okay. He was taking a step up.

So Fred was a veteran union man. He was also a good friend to the hardworking ladies of Copeland Oaks and quite unashamed of his support for their union effort, his wife's managerial loyalty notwithstanding. I didn't pick up on Fred's empathy with the workers during my interviews with him before the election—he was a good poker player, apparently. I knew he wasn't carrying out my orders to interrogate his eleven subordinates on their union sympathies; and he sure wasn't doing any lobbying on management's behalf. But Fred was such a cranky guy, independent in that defiant, midwestern, blue-collar sort of way. I figured his stubbornness was just his nature, and although I tormented him about it endlessly during our one-on-one interviews, I didn't let it worry me much. Whatever sympathy Fred had for the organizing effort he kept quiet; he even joined the other managers in signing my final anti-union letter.

But after the union win, Fred let his views be known: the union had won, for God's sake, now let it go about its business. Fred refused to comply with my post-election directive to snub union supporters. "I'll talk to whoever I want to," was his gruff retort. Fred did more than talk. When he passed union organizers in the hallways and on the grounds, he was always sure to give them a thumbs-up: "Way to go! I don't blame you for what you're doing. It's about time. You deserve it. Keep up the good work."

Fred's outspokenness annoyed me, to be sure, but not as much as it annoyed Claude Roe. I saw Fred as a loudmouth; Claude saw him as a Judas. As time went on, Claude became more rabid and more irrational in his contempt for Fred. Dr. Roe, who was most self-consciously patrician under usual circumstances, became suddenly and uncharacteristically rash whenever the conversation turned to his maintenance man. The minister's ire bubbled over into the most inarticulate and decidedly un-Christian accusations, peppered with raw expletives. I delighted in these lapses of self-control and enjoyed baiting him on the subject: I listened as he speculated on how Fred must have collaborated with union organizers, and I joined him in defiling the traitor. To me, those conversations were pure entertainment and not to be taken seriously. I liked Fred. Claude, however, had never been more serious, and he was building his case.

Where the payoff theory came from, I do not know. On March 25, 1981, Claude called me into his office to inform me that he believed Fred Moracco had been on the Local 47 payroll. I knew what that meant, of course: Fred was to be fired.

A little before four that afternoon, Claude summoned Fred to his office. When his maintenance man appeared, the reverend Claude pushed a sheet of paper and a pen across his desk and dryly ordered Fred to sign it. It was a resignation letter.

Fred read the words on the page, looked quizzically at Claude, and refused. He had no desire to resign, and Claude had given him no reason why he should. Fine, said Claude. Then you're fired. Get out. As of now you are trespassing.

The next day Anna quit in protest of her husband's ill treatment.

Claude did not choose to share with Fred the reasons for his sudden dismissal. He did share them, however, with the rest of the Copeland work force and with the public at large. A few days after the firing, he called a meeting of employees and residents. He confirmed that one of the department heads had been let go and, using a parable as his cover, implied that the miscreant had been stealing from the company. Over the next few days vague references to theft solidified into a specific charge, and soon everyone was debating whether or not it was true that Fred Moracco had stolen $13,000. Within weeks all the newspapers in northeastern Ohio had carried the story.

After the fourth negotiating session I knew it was time for some new ammunition; the stalling tactic was wearing thin. I got a lucky break. It so happened that Local 47's patience was also wearing thin, and I heard through my network that the union would soon hold a strike vote. Well, nothing makes as sweet music to the ears of anti-union management as the word strike—particularly in the fall of 1981. In August of that year the most powerful man in the world, the president of the United States of America, had pulled off the biggest union bust in history. That month President Ronald Reagan fired thirteen thousand striking federal air traffic controllers—who were striking essentially for safer working conditions— and allowed their employers to hire permanent replacements. Reagan also had five union leaders prosecuted under a never-before-used law prohibiting strikes against the government. In firing the strikers, and calling their leaders criminals, the president, himself a former union official as onetime president of the Screen Actors Guild, displayed his contempt for organized labor. The firing annihilated the air controllers union, PATCO, and crippled all labor organizations by destroying their most powerful economic weapon, the strike. What I did not know was that a few months later, Reagan would outlaw PATCO itself. Thus, in ninety days Ronald Reagan recast the crimes of union busting as acts of patriotism. When word came to me of Local 47's strike vote, I grinned. I knew the moves. And I would start making them immediately.

I called an urgent supervisors meeting to get the word out about the union's dastardly plan. This is what I told my audience: "Many of you may have heard that the union is considering calling a strike. It should come as no surprise, that's what we've been saying would happen all along." The supervisors nodded but kept their wide eyes on me. They knew more was coming. "What may come as a surprise is that only the people who signed union authorization cards have been invited to vote." My congregation gasped. "That's right. Now why do you think they would do that?" I asked with a smarmy tone.

The indignation was palpable. Even the LPNs, many of whom had managed to hold on to their ideals and keep their friendships throughout the crusade, looked grief stricken. Could it be true? Could they have been wrong about the union?

It was true—half-true. True, only workers who had signed authorization cards eight months earlier would be allowed to vote. Also true, however, was a very compelling reason, which I did not mention: the law. Only union members are allowed by law to vote on union issues. And until a contract is signed and membership dues collected, only signatories of the authorization cards are considered by law to be members. The fact was, the union had no choice about who got to vote and who didn't; it was only doing what it was legally bound to do. The inference I knew my congregation would draw, however, was that the union was trying to stack the vote in favor of a strike by allowing only pro-union people to cast ballots. The union representatives, who were sixty miles away in Cleveland, had a hard time countering my charges.

That fire ignited, I went about developing a "strike contingency plan." Such a plan purports to set up a system so that vital business operations can continue if workers walk off the job. Sounds reasonable and benign. In truth, strike contingency plans have but one dual aim: to scare the workers and rout the union. My plan would scare the workers all right—scare them into thinking a strike would be dangerous; scare them into believing a strike would be prolonged; scare them into thinking a strike would be futile; scare them into believing strikers would lose their jobs. That was my plan. Once again the workers would be made to feel they could not possibly win.

I hit on all fronts. To show that Copeland was preparing for a long strike, I had Claude run Help Wanted ads in all the local town newspapers. We wanted workers to know that the moment they walked out the door, plenty of eager job seekers would walk right in behind them. I got the word out on the grapevine that Claude already had a backlog of applications and that he had started interviews. The message was not lost on the Copeland work force. Since most of the employees who would be striking held unskilled positions, they knew their jobs would not be hard to fill. They began to worry.

My next move was to tighten security around Copeland, a clear indication that management expected the strike to be violent. At my direction Claude installed bright lamps in the unlit employee parking lot. He told supervisors directly that the lights were being added for the protection of workers, due to the increasing hostility of the union. Claude assured his worried supervisors that a security force would be hired in the event of a strike to protect supervisors and those workers who chose to continue working rather than join the rabble on the pavement. In my most cunning antistrike play, I convinced Claude to buy an old school bus, to be used to shuttle loyal employees safely across the picket line. We let supervisors know—and they let their subordinates know—that anyone who wanted to work through the strike would be picked up, taken to work, and driven home in the Copeland bus. That way they would not have to drive alone past angry picketers or leave their cars to be vandalized in the employee parking lot. We even drew up a dozen alternate routes to employees' communities, so that the bus could take a different course each day—sort of like a moving missile plan—and thus evade any enterprising union people who might want to show up at the stops to try to talk the workers out of boarding. The employees worried a little more.

Finally I dispatched maintenance workers to paint a white line at the edge of Copeland property, a line picketers would not be allowed to cross. Companies do not have to allow strikers to picket on their property, and Copeland certainly did not intend to. As it turned out, Copeland property stretched all the way to the end of the long driveway. Since there was no sidewalk, the white line put the picket zone in the street. The strikers would have to share the road with cars and the occasional bus and truck.

With all but one round of my contingency plan fired, I began hearing talk about union supporters trying to enlist friends to carry picket signs for them. They were very worried now. We sat back and waited.

About nine months after bargaining had begun, Local 47 asked its newest membership for authorization to call a strike. The Copeland voters overwhelmingly approved. A month later union reps notified us that the workers planned to walk out. Labor law requires unions to give health care facilities ten days advance notice of a strike so that the institution can arrange for meals and vital care for patients or, if that is impossible on site, transfer patients to other facilities. Ten days was plenty of time for me to unleash the final phase of the strike contingency plan. That's when I called a meeting with the residents committee.

Claude and I made our point of view clear: those nasty union people were planning to abandon the sweet old ladies for the picket line, we said. They wanted more money, and it looked as though they would stop at nothing to get it. Well, we wanted the residents to know that management would do everything it could to protect them from the unpleasantness. But they also needed to be aware of how to protect themselves. Besides keeping their doors locked and their valuables hidden, the residents should not engage in any unnecessary conversation with the union workers. Some of the union people were a little crazy, we confided; we couldn't be sure they wouldn't abuse the elderly folks if it suited their cause. For that reason we would see to it that no resident would ever be left alone and unprotected with a pro-union employee. As that message was being duly disseminated by the residents committee, Claude sent his own letter to all residents, apologizing for any worry the union strife was causing them and assuring them of management's abiding concern for their well-being.

At 7:00 a.m. on strike day, as the morning shift was due to come on, management took its battle stations and braced itself for the assault. Poof! Nothing happened. No one walked out. The day dragged on. No one showed up with picket signs. No one. Strike day came and went; it was the quietest day Copeland Oaks had ever known.

Nine down, three to go.

On the heels of the strike that wasn't there, I got a call from the union. We were nine months into negotiations and nowhere; would I consider meeting with a federal mediator? Hell, it was fine by me. I said sure, I'd go to the damn meeting. I knew the federal mediation system was bullshit, so I wasn't worried. The idea is laudable, I suppose. The mediator is supposed to meet separately with each side, find some common ground, then bring them together and bless the marriage. But the joke is that the mediator can do nothing to compel agreement. He has no authority, no power, no force of law behind him. I spent a day at the federal building in Akron going for cups of coffee with the mediator and my committee. It just used up time and maybe made me look as though I were really trying. Meanwhile the clock went tick, tick, tick.

In November 1981 preparations were begun for the opening of the adjacent Crandall Medical Center, the construction of which was nearly complete. The new medical facility was to bring with it an expansion of Copeland's traditional mission and heighten both the prestige and income of the Sebring retirement community. Employees were as eager as Dr. Roe to cut the ribbon. What no one but I knew was that Crandall was a booby trap. From the beginning Crandall had been talked about as a company distinct from Copeland and was, in fact, separately incorporated. The point was made early and often in the Copeland campaign that Crandall would not just be an extension of Copeland Oaks. Indeed, the letterhead I had used for Claude's "Dear Staff Member" letters listed the names of both institutions, followed by the written elbow jab, "two separate and independent legal entities." It had been my argument, fully supported by Lou Davies, that should Copeland Oaks somehow go union, Crandall could still be preserved as Claude's union-free rumpus room. It was a different company. Now the time had come to make use of that carefully guarded distinction.

With the opening of the medical center one month away, Copeland management began the task of staffing the facility. The job vacancies were heavily advertised in the area press, and Copeland employees were welcome to apply—along with the rest of northeastern Ohio. Copeland employees were told that since Crandall was a separate corporation they should not expect to be hired there automatically. At my insistence, Copeland employees wishing to work at Crandall were required to fill out job applications like everyone else and join the competition. Even workers whose jobs were being transferred to the medical building next door had to apply for the "new" Crandall positions, which, of course, were non-union jobs.

It was a scam. I designed the Copeland-Crandall shuffle, specifically to get rid of unwanted—read "pro-union"—workers. In fact, almost fifty Copeland jobs were to be transferred to Crandall, including all dietary positions, all laundry, most of the nursing, and some housekeeping. The jobs were moved, but at my direction the executive director of Crandall, who happened to be a certain Claude L. Roe, slyly refused to let the people who held those jobs go with them.

The union cried foul over the transfer game. Officials argued, rightfully so, that Copeland and Crandall were clearly one company, regardless of the legal technicalities. The jobs being transferred to Crandall would remain essentially the same as they were at Copeland, they said, and the bosses would be the same. In protest of the ploy, union officers advised members not to fill out job applications. It was a mistake, but not one that really mattered, since we would have gotten what we wanted either way. As jobs were moved to Crandall, the corresponding positions at Copeland were eliminated. Suddenly a nurse's aide or housekeeper would find herself unemployed. She could fill out an application for Crandall and maybe get hired there—or maybe not. Or she could refuse to fill out an application, as several of the strongest union supporters did, and lose her job for certain.

One nurse's aide, a forty-two-year-old single mother named Winnie Waithman, decided to play the game and fill out an application. She was told there was no job for her at Crandall. All the medical positions had been filled. Funny thing: Winnie just happened to be an inside organizer, election observer, member of the negotiating committee, and designated union spokesperson.

"The ones of us they didn't want over there, the 'undesirables,' were told there was no place for us," Winnie says plainly.

The big day came in December 1981. Crandall opened its doors, and eighteen Copeland employees lost their jobs.

Meanwhile, a hand-picked committee of anti-union workers began circulating a petition calling for a vote to remove Local 47 as their bargaining representative. Thirty percent of the rank-and-file workers signed, and the decertification petition reached Region 8 of the NLRB before Christmas.

Ten down, two to go.

The NLRB regional director had barely begun looking over the decertification petition in the early days of 1982 when he received a package of legal forms from Local 47. In the package were twenty unfair labor practice charges against Copeland Oaks. The union accused the company of bad-faith bargaining, refusal to bargain, and eighteen counts of firing an employee for union-related activities.

The charges worried Claude. He was counting on the decertification election to bury the union once and for all. His hopes faded when he received the notice of the charges and the admonition that the decertification petition would not be considered until all unfair labor practice charges were resolved. He summoned Lou Davies and me, turning first to Lou and pleading with him to defend Copeland.

Lou would not be moved from his Pontius Pilot stance: "Claude, I know Marty's been surface bargaining. How can I go in there and defend Copeland against charges of which I know it's guilty? I can't do it."

Claude next looked at me. No, I couldn't argue law before the NLRB, but I could help. Since I hadn't been needed around Copeland Oaks much lately, I had managed to pick up a couple of other union-busting jobs. Through one of the companies, Cyberex Inc., an electronics manufacturer in Mentor, Ohio, I had met an attorney. He was sharp, he was tough, and he owed me. I told Claude I was sure he'd be glad to take on the work. He was Earl Leiken, the eggheaded lawyer who would ride with me in half a dozen union busts over the next four years, including the bash at Cravat Coal.

The NLRB suspended the decertification petition and set a hearing on the first two of the string of unfair labor practice charges pending against Copeland. It began with the bad-faith bargaining charges. The board sent agents out to Copeland to interview everyone who had been in on the bargaining sessions and a number of people who had not. As the investigation plodded along, I found myself getting uncharacteristically nervous. I was beginning to doubt that we could win this one; my hostility and intransigence at the bargaining table had been pretty transparent. I had rarely even planned a move. It was all off the cuff. Maybe the board would see through it.

Luckily for me, I had President Reagan on my side—again. During his first year in office Reagan had filled the NLRB and its regional agencies with pro-management members. The president had also slashed the board's budget, making it difficult for agents to carry out full, lengthy investigations. All that made it harder than ever for unions to convince the board to issue unfair labor practice complaints.

With those clear advantages, Earl went to bat. In his unspectacular style he won a most spectacular victory. Using the few morsels I gave him—like the fact that I had initialed off on several contract items and the fact that I had agreed to meet with the federal mediator—he concocted a solid defense. The union members reported what they saw and heard, but, amazingly, it wasn't enough to prove that the company had no intention of reaching a contract. The board dismissed the charges.

Eleven down, one to go.

The union's twelve months were up in February 1982. The NLRB was still scratching its way through the unjust firing charges, but I was no longer needed. Negotiations had been suspended. I moved on to work my scam at other companies in northern Ohio, leaving it to Earl Leiken to finish the Copeland bloodletting.

I was a happy man. My nineteen-month part-time stint at Copeland had netted me $160,000.

In March 1983 the eighteen women who lost their jobs in the Copeland-Crandall shuffle won their case. The NLRB issued eighteen complaints against the company, ruling that the employees had been fired in retaliation for their union activities. The board ordered reinstatement and full back pay for all. Only one of the eighteen fired employees, Winnie Waithman, chose to return to her job. The same month as the board ruling she was hired back as a nurse's aide at Crandall Medical Center. The reason for her return: "They said I'd never be back. I wanted to show them."

But it was already too late for Local 47. By that time the union had given up. As the unfair labor practice hearings had dragged on, the union's chances of winning in a decertification election— which would be reactivated with the resolution of the firings—had grown dimmer and dimmer. Its strongest allies had long since been fired or promoted or had quit, and scores of new, carefully screened employees were now cleaning the sheets and changing the bedpans of Copeland and Crandall residents. Hardly anyone was left who believed in the union, and even the believers' faith had been badly shaken. Local 47 had given nearly three years to the Copeland effort, invested thousands of hours of staff time, and spent tens of thousands of dollars, and still a contract between Local 47 and Claude L. Roe seemed as remote as it had in the autumn of 1980.

Joe Murphy decided to pull the plug. On December 6, 1982, Local 47 filed with the NLRB a brief form called a "disclaimer of interest." With that, the union walked away from Copeland Oaks and cut its losses in Sebring, Ohio.

A decade after the union election, Jim Horton, Art Worthy, and Joe Murphy had all retired from Local 47. Claude Roe, Bill Hogg, and Kathleen Taylor had retired from Copeland Oaks. Judy Stanley was married, had a daughter, and was doing PR for the Copeland admittance office. Jean Householder was working as a factory seamstress at a non-union company. Phil Ganni had died. Winnie Waithman was still a nurse's aide at Crandall Medical Center. She was making $5.97 an hour, and she still had no union.

As for Fred Moracco, his life was ruined. Copeland's antiunion campaign not only cost him his job, pension benefits, health coverage, and life insurance, it had also cost him his future. Fred sued Claude Roe and Copeland Oaks for $2.8 million for firing him without just cause and for defaming his character. As the lawsuit ground through the legal system, Fred underwent major surgery, watched his diabetes intensify—he believes due to the stress— and his eyesight deteriorate. For a while he hunted for employment, but it was hopeless. In interview after interview he was asked to explain what had happened at his last job; over and over he told the story. He never worked again.

Anna got a nursing job at Alliance Hospital and for ten years— until her back gave out—was able to support her ailing husband. At the judge's insistence, Fred's lawsuit was eventually settled out of court, for what Fred calls "a pittance." He cannot elaborate because of a nondisclosure rule in the settlement, but he offers that the dollars have brought little comfort to a sick, half-blind old man.

Does this chapter help understand why union bargaining takes so long?

Have you heard the company tell stories blaming the Union for the lack of progress?

Have you wondered why negotiating is taking so long?

Did you see even a single example of the Union being greedy in their demands in this chapter?

Have you seen those the company likes get better schedules?

Wearing people down is a prime method used by union busters. Will you endure?

*This Special Edition has selected chapters
from the original book*

A Union Buster Confesses
By
Martin Jay Levitt

Available from Amazon.com in both a print and Kindle edition.

*For more details, more examples, and a complete understanding
of the life of Martin Jay Levitt, buy the complete book.*

*For feedback about this Special Edition, or to inquire about a
Special Edition tailored specifically for your cause, email*

ConfessionsSE@39PageGuideBooks.com